SAILING SHIPS

of the Maritimes

SAILING SHIPS

of the Maritimes

AN ILLUSTRATED HISTORY
OF SHIPPING AND SHIPBUILDING
IN THE MARITIME PROVINCES OF CANADA
1750–1925

CHARLES A. ARMOUR & THOMAS LACKEY

McGraw-Hill Ryerson Limited

Toronto   Montreal   New York   London   Sydney   Johannesburg
Mexico   Panama   Düsseldorf   Singapore   São Paulo
Kuala Lumpur   New Delhi

SAILING SHIPS OF THE MARITIMES

ISBN 0-07-077756-x

1 2 3 4 5 6 7 8 9 10 BP 4 3 2 1 0 9 8 7 6 5

Design by Maher & Garbutt

Printed and bound in Canada

Acknowledgments

We would like to acknowledge the help and cooperation of the directors and staff of the various museums, archives and libraries as well as private individuals who made available paintings, plans, books, manuscript material and notes. We would also like to thank the various institutions and private individuals who gave us permission to reproduce photographs in the book and to quote manuscript sources.

In addition, we wish to thank the Albert County Museum of Hopewell, Mr. George Bates of Halifax, Miss Phyllis Blakeley of Halifax, Miss Susan Buggey of Ottawa, Mr. James Creighton of Dartmouth, Mr. Robert Dimock of Dartmouth, Mr. Basil Greenhill of London, England; Dr. Del Muise of Ottawa, Miss Patricia Ney of Halifax, Mr. Graham Opie of Halifax, Mr. Dennis Pulley of Halifax, Dr. Thomas Raddall of Liverpool, Mr. and Mrs. Richard Rice of Montreal, Mr. James Snowdon of Fredericton, Mr. Michael Sultzbach of West Chester, Pennsylvania, U.S.A.; Miss Grace Tratt of Halifax, Mr. Robert Treleaven of Halifax, Mr. Jeff Wright of Fredericton and the numerous people throughout the Maritimes whom we interviewed during the past two summers.

Finally we wish to extend a special thanks to Mr. Niels Jannasch of the Nova Scotia Museum, who answered our endless questions; Captain Kai Böggild and Mr. John Bigelow of Halifax, who gave valuable advice on the technical details; Mrs. Marion Böggild of Halifax, who read the entire text and made many helpful suggestions; Miss Gertrude Tratt of Halifax, who helped proofread the manuscript and Miss Hedy Böggild of Halifax, who typed much of the original draft and did a considerable amount of editing.

Contents

Introduction

From such an unfavourable climate as that of Nova Scotia° very little can be expected. For seven months the cold is intense and the remaining part of the year the heat becomes as unsupportable as the cold was before and the country is wrapt in a constant gloom of fog.

This country is almost one continuous forest and agriculture, though attempted by the English settlers has hitherto made very little progress. In most parts, the soil is thin and barren, the corn it produces of a shrivled kind, like rye, and the grass is intermixed with a cold spungy moss. Not withstanding this general barrenness, the soil in some parts is extremely fertile. It is, for the most, well adapted to the produce of Hemp and Flax. The timber is of a fine nature for Ship-building, and produces Pitch and Tar.[1]

When Sir Charles Whitworth wrote this description of Nova Scotia in 1773, the Maritime Provinces of Canada were, for the most part, a vast wilderness of trees with only a few scattered settlements along the coast. Less than one hundred years later Canada had developed a vast shipbuilding industry that during the peak years of the 1860s supplied nearly one-third of all British shipping. By the end of the century over 26,000 vessels had been built in the Maritimes. While many of these were built for direct transfer to British owners, many Maritime merchants owned and operated their own vessels. In 1878, the peak year in Canadian ownership, Canada stood fifth on the list of ship-owning countries of the world, and 7,469 vessels totalling 1,333,015 tons were on the registry books. Of this number, 4,467 vessels, representing 943,583 tons, were registered in the Maritime Provinces.[2]

The first sharp increase in shipbuilding in the Maritimes occurred during the Napoleonic Wars. The period from 1820 to 1826 marked the beginning of the great timber trade and a subsequent boom in shipbuilding. A further increase occurred in 1840. The beginning of free trade in 1844, the California Gold Rush of 1849, the discovery of gold in Australia in 1851, the outbreak of the Crimean War in 1854 and the American Civil War in 1861 all resulted in periods of great shipbuilding activity. In the peak year, 1865, more than 660 vessels were built.

The close of the American Civil War in 1865 and the end of Reciprocity marked the decline of the great wooden shipbuilding era. Except for a brief resurgence in the 1870s and 1880s, the wooden sailing ship was gradually giving way to the iron steamship. During the early years of the twentieth century small schooners for fishing and coastal trade continued to be built. The years during and immediately following the First World War saw a revival in shipbuilding and the peak period of the three- and four-masted schooner.

° In 1773 Nova Scotia included all of what is now Nova Scotia and New Brunswick and part of Maine.

With the exception of very small craft, Government regulations required that all vessels be registered. Any serious study of shipbuilding, therefore, necessitates the searching of the original shipping registers. While the majority of these have survived, many of the eighteenth and early nineteenth century shipping registers are missing. It has been possible, however, to reconstruct many of these records from other sources.

One of the most difficult problems facing the researcher is that of finding the name of the shipbuilder. Since the "builder" may be the owner of the shipyard, the master builder or the foreman in charge, different sources may give different names. From 1824 to 1854, and from 1874 onwards, the builder's name is usually given on the Shipping Register. Unfortunately, the names are not usually given between 1855 and 1873, the period of greatest shipbuilding activity. Other sources include the commercial shipping registers (Lloyd's Register, Bureau Veritas, Record of American Shipping, etc.), newspaper accounts of launchings, family papers and business records. However, many vessels never appear in the commercial registers; the launchings of most vessels are not recorded in the newspapers and the records of only a few shipbuilders and shipping companies have survived. In many cases, therefore, it is impossible to obtain a complete list of the vessels constructed by a particular builder or, in some cases, even to determine when he started building.

The illustrations throughout the book are contemporary oil paintings, watercolours, engravings, documents, plans and photographs. They have been selected so as to give as wide a representation as possible to the various types of vessels and to builders in various areas at different times. Unfortunately, many important builders and companies are not represented, either because of lack of space or because no illustrations of their vessels are available. The text accompanying the illustrations not only describes each vessel but briefly traces the growth and development of shipping and shipbuilding in the Maritimes and shows the evolution of ship design and rigging changes. Where possible, contemporary manuscript sources have been used. Logbooks, diaries, correspondence, business records, official documents and newspapers have been quoted in order to show, not only the romance of the sea, but also the hardships, frustrations, humour and tragedy of life on board a sailing ship.

The Eighteenth Century

Because many of the eighteenth century shipping records have been destroyed, this period of shipbuilding activity has been almost completely ignored. However, fragments of early records have survived. A Naval Office return for Canso, Nova Scotia, listing vessels that cleared that port from May to December 1730 indicates that vessels were being registered at Canso and Annapolis Royal as early as 1728.

On July 19, 1749, within a month of the arrival of Cornwallis and the new settlers, a Naval Office was opened at Halifax. Records of this office, which extend to 1765, give detailed information on vessels entering and clearing the harbour.[1] Although most of the vessels were registered at New York, Boston or other New England ports, the lists give the names of 180 vessels registered at Halifax during this period, as well as a small number registered at Annapolis Royal and Louisbourg. Many of these vessels had been built in New England or were French or Spanish prizes condemned in the Court of Vice Admiralty at Halifax. However, after 1755 an increasing number of the vessels being registered in Nova Scotia were built in the province.

The period from 1749 onwards saw a relatively rapid population growth. Special impetus was given by the arrival of the Lunenburg settlers (1750–52), the New England planters (1760), the *Hector* settlers (1773), the Yorkshire settlers (1774) and the Loyalists (1782–84). The result was the establishment of major settlements at Halifax, Saint John and Shelburne as well as many other ports along the coast of Nova Scotia and Prince Edward Island. New Brunswick was created a separate province in 1784, and Saint John was established as a port of registry. These communities quickly developed active trade with the West Indies and Great Britain, and shipbuilding soon became a major industry.

In 1786 "A Bill for the Further Increase and Encouragement of Shipping and Navigation"[2] was passed in the British Parliament. There were two main clauses that most affected Canadian shipping: (1) "All and every vessel having a deck or being of the burden of 15 tons upward belonging to any of H.M. Subjects" was required to be registered. (2) No foreign vessels including any vessels "built in the North American colony now called United States of America" were allowed to be registered except those captured and condemned as lawful prizes. This second clause caused a storm of protest from many of "His Majesties Loyal Subjects" who had fled from "His Majesties Rebellious Colonies" and now found that they were unable to register their American-built vessels. The Court of St. James was bombarded with petitions requesting relief from this disregard of their loyalty.[3] The Court quietly granted their petitions.

On February 13, 1787, the following notice appeared in the *Nova Scotia Gazette*:

This is further to notify the Owners and Masters of Ships and vessels owned in this Province, as well Coasting and Fishing vessels as Others, being the Burden of 15 tons or upwards, that from

A View of the Entrance of Petit Passage

From *The Atlantic Neptune* by J. F. W. Des Barres.
Engraved by H. Ashby, 1779.
Courtesy of the Dalhousie University Library,
Halifax, N.S. William Inglis Morse Collection.

The large vessel on the left is a merchant ship of the mid-eighteenth century. The other vessels are schooners of various sizes.

and after the first Day of March ensuing, they must be registered according to the late Act of Parliament — otherwise they will be liable to the Penalties mentioned in said act.

Halifax, Feb. 8, 1787

With the introduction of the new Navigation Act in 1787, five ports of registry were established in the Maritime Provinces: Saint John, St. John's Island (later Prince Edward Island), Port Roseway (later Shelburne), Halifax and Sydney, Cape Breton. The shipping registers for Prince Edward Island and Sydney have survived from 1787 onwards. Unfortunately, most of the registers before 1817 for Saint John, Halifax and Shelburne have been destroyed. Not only were many of the Plantation Copies of the Colonial Shipping Registers destroyed in the London Custom House fire of 1814, but other valuable records, including port lists and annual lists, were lost as well.

However, copies of a few of the shipping registers are extant. Scattered copies of Annual Lists for British Colonial ports and Naval Office returns for many Canadian and West Indies ports have been found. English and Scottish shipping registers also give details of many Maritime-built vessels. These records have made it possible to reconstruct many of the eighteenth and early nineteenth century shipping lists and shipping registers for New Brunswick and Nova Scotia.

From 1787 until the end of the century, official records indicate that over 700 vessels were built in the Maritime Provinces. Many large ships and brigs of over 200 and 300 tons were constructed. While many of these were intended for immediate sale in England, and Scotland, some were locally owned. In 1799, 721 vessels, giving a total of nearly 37,000 tons, were registered in the Maritimes. An extensive fleet of small schooners, brigantines and brigs was actively engaged, not only in local but also in West Indies and European trade. A shipbuilding industry, which was to continue for almost a hundred years, had been established.

The Atlantic Neptune

In 1763 Joseph Frederick Wallet Des Barres was engaged by the British Admiralty to undertake a detailed survey of the coast of Nova Scotia and the American Colonies. While many of the early surveys were completed by Des Barres himself, he was later assisted by Major Samuel Holland who did much of the work after Des Barres returned to England in 1774. In England, Des Barres began the detailed task of revising, editing and illustrating the charts for publication. They were published in 1777 under the title *The Atlantic Neptune*.

Apart from the charts themselves, many of the volumes contain extremely fine views of ports and harbours of the Maritime Provinces, and give a wealth of detail of the types of vessels that would have been found around the coast at that time.

This illustration shows a Des Barres map of Halifax Harbour and two late eighteenth century navigational instruments: on the left is a Hadley's reflecting quadrant, or octant, and on the right, a ring dial. The sketches along the bottom show the approaches to Halifax, and in the centre is a set of sailing directions for entering the harbour.

While commissioned by the British Admiralty for use by the Royal Navy, the charts in *The Atlantic Neptune* became the standard guide for all ships along the Atlantic coast during the late eighteenth and early nineteenth centuries. More detailed surveying projects in the nineteenth century, coupled with more advanced hydrographic techniques, produced charts of greater accuracy which gradually superseded the charts in *The Atlantic Neptune*.

Eighteenth century map and nautical instruments

Chart of Halifax Harbour.
From *The Atlantic Neptune*
by J. F. W. Des Barres.
Engraved by H. Ashby, 1776.

It is almost impossible to say with any degree of certainty which was the "first" vessel or "first" ship built in a particular area during this period. A few of the early vessels built in the Maritimes are listed below. The information has been compiled from official sources.

The *Medford*, a schooner of 20 tons, was built at Annapolis Royal in 1745, registered at Boston on November 23, 1749, and owned by John Richardson. Records show she was trading between Halifax and Boston in 1751.

The *Osborn Gally*, a brig of 100 tons, was built and registered at Halifax in 1751 and owned by John Gorham. A contemporary port list gives an interesting example of the cargo carried by a colonial ship. The vessel cleared Halifax on July 8, 1751, with "Sam'l Appleton" as master and a crew of six men, bound for London with a cargo of ". . . 80 tons of Black Birch Timber, 313 oars, 240 Hand Spikes, 70 spars, 3136 Qt. blubber, 3 tuns Pitch Pine and 20 Qt. fish."[4]

The *Swan*, a schooner of 15 tons, was built at Halifax in 1750, registered at Halifax on April 18, 1753, and owned by Benjamin Gerrish.

The *Recovery*, a two-deck ship of 173 tons, was built in Nova Scotia in 1781 and registered at London May 11, 1787. Its dimensions, given on the London register, were: length, 85 feet 6 inches; breadth, 22 feet 3 inches.

The *Alfred Frigate*, a two-deck ship of 294 tons, was built "on the Island of Saint Johns, N.B." in 1785 and registered at London August 28, 1788. Its dimensions were: length, 100 feet, 6 inches; breadth, 27 feet, 11 inches.

The *Lord Sheffield*, a ship of 130 tons, was built on the Saint John River by Nehemiah Beckwith in 1786. The vessel was registered at Saint John on August 24, 1786, and owned by Benedict Arnold.

Annapolis Royal

Originally founded in 1604 and named Port Royal by de Monts and Champlain, the name was changed to Annapolis when it was captured by the British in 1710. Eventually it became known as Annapolis Royal and from 1710 to 1749 was the capital of Nova Scotia. While very little is known about the extent of shipbuilding in the Maritimes under French rule, it is recorded that the first vessels built in New France were two small craft launched at Port Royal by François Grave in 1606.

This view shows the town and harbour of Annapolis Royal with a variety of one- and two-masted vessels of the period. The large ship in the centre is a British Admiralty vessel, probably the one carrying Des Barres' survey crew. One of the three men in the left foreground is engaged in sketching the harbour approaches, perhaps for a Des Barres map.

A View of Annapolis Royal

From *The Atlantic Neptune*
by J. F. W. Des Barres.
Engraved by H. Ashby, 1779.

1787–1792

In 1787 Shelburne was established as one of the three ports of registry for Nova Scotia. Most of the vessels registered there were built in Shelburne, Argyle, Yarmouth, Barrington or other ports along the south shore of Nova Scotia. The majority of these were small schooners, brigantines and brigs, locally owned and actively involved in the coastal, fishing and West Indies trade.

The *Nova Scotia Gazette* for January 9, 1787, gave this account of the launching of the ship *Roseway* in late December, 1786:

Shelburne, December 28
On Friday last was launched from the shipyard above King Street, the beautiful ship ROSEWAY, about two hundred and fifty tons burden, built for Messrs M'Lean and Bogle, of this town, Merchants. This is the First Ship that was launched in this province since its first settlement, and of good stuff, excellent workmanship, strength and a handsome model, are recommendations in a vessel, she will do no little credit to the Builder and the settlement of Shelburne.

Newspaper reports of the eighteenth century appear to have exaggerated the facts much as they do today: the tonnage of the *Roseway* was in fact 181. The vessel was registered at Shelburne on May 5, 1787, and owned by Peter Bogle & Co. The *Roseway* was registered at London on February 4, 1789, and owned at that port until she was lost on January 29, 1793. Her dimensions, given in the London register, were: length, 78 feet; breadth, 23 feet 10 inches and 5 feet 6 inches between decks.

A number of large vessels, built at Sissiboo, Saint Mary's Bay, Annapolis County, were registered at Shelburne and almost immediately transferred to the London registry. The largest was the *Governor Wentworth*, a ship of 325 tons built in 1792, registered at Shelburne on July 11, 1792, and transferred to London the following year. Her dimensions were: length, 102 feet 5 inches; breadth, 28 feet 3 inches. The vessel remained on the London register until she was lost in 1802.

Shipbuilding in Prince Edward Island and Cape Breton Island during the eighteenth century was confined mainly to small shallops, schooners and brigantines. Nearly all were built for the local coasting and fishing trade and only a few were sent to England. Prince Edward Island vessels were built at Grand Rustico, Savage Harbour, New London, Bay of Fortune and Vernon River. The names of John Cambridge, John Hill and Arthur Owen appear frequently as owners in the early registers.

Cape Breton shipbuilding was mainly centred around Arichat and Isle Madame, and an extensive fleet of small vessels was operating out of this area. As early as 1766, Charles Robin of Jersey was operating out of Paspebiac on the Gaspé, and a few years later extended his operation to Cheticamp and Arichat. By 1787 John Janvrin & Company, from Guernsey, were also established at Arichat.

In the centre of the engraving is an eighteenth century brigantine. The vessel differs from the mid-nineteenth century brigantine in having a square topsail on the mainmast. The vessel on the left is a single-topsail schooner and the large vessel on the right is a ship. The size of these vessels can be estimated from the figures on deck. It must be remembered that many craft of this size traded regularly across the Atlantic.

The North Entrance of Grand Passage (detail)

From *The Atlantic Neptune*
by J. F. W. Des Barres.
Engraved by H. Ashby, 1779.

Courtesy of the Dalhousie
University Library, Halifax, N.S.
William Inglis Morse Collection.

A local merchant who was beginning to build for himself and for British owners was William Lowden. During the American Revolution Lowden had begun trading with Pictou and he moved his family there in 1788. The *Royal Gazette* for November 13, 1798, gives an account of the launching of the ship *Harriet* on October 24:

> Pictou, Oct'r 25, 1798
>
> Yesterday was launched here, by Messrs. Lowden's, the Ship HARRIET; burden 600 Tons. She is pierced for 24 guns, and supposed to be the largest and finest ship built in this province. Her bottom is composed of oak and black birch timber, and her upper works, beams &c., totally of pitch pine; on account of which mode of construction, she is said to be little inferior in quality to British built ships; and does peculiar credit, not only to this growing settlement, but to the province at large.

While this vessel appears to have been the largest built in Nova Scotia up to that time, the newspaper has again exaggerated the size. When the ship was registered at Halifax on October 3, 1798, the tonnage was given as 422. The ship had two decks and measured 110 feet in length and 30 feet 4 inches in breadth.* The owners were Samuel, William, Thomas, Robert and David Lowden. On March 18, 1800, the *Harriet* was registered at Liverpool, England, and was then owned by Michael Humble, Samuel Holland and Nicholas Hurry. She was sold to other merchants in Liverpool in 1810 and was lost in 1819.

Humble, Holland and Hurry of Liverpool, in partnership with James Fraser and James Thom of Halifax, had begun purchasing Maritime vessels in 1798. During the early years of the nineteenth century a number of vessels were built for them in Miramichi, New Brunswick. While these vessels were initially registered at Saint John or Halifax, they were immediately transferred to Liverpool, England.

One of the many merchants in New Brunswick was John Black who had established himself in Saint John. As early as 1788 he was operating in partnership with James Hunter and George Robertson of Greenock, and William Forsyth and William Smith of Halifax. Most of their vessels were built in Saint John and a few in Nova Scotia. This company holds the distinction of having built in Saint John two of the largest vessels constructed in the Maritimes at that time. The *America*, a ship of 566 tons, was built in 1796. The vessel had two decks and measured 124 feet in length and 32 feet 5 inches in breadth. The *Duke of Kent*, a ship of 708 tons, was built in 1799.

While many of the company's vessels were transferred immediately to Greenock, both of these vessels remained registered at Saint John and were operated by John Black & Co. The *America* was sold at Plymouth and registered there in 1811. The *Duke of Kent* was lost off Grand Manan on November 10, 1809. It was to be another twenty years before a vessel of over 500 tons was built in New Brunswick.

Some of the problems encountered by a shipbuilder in 1800 are revealed in this advertisement which appeared in the *St. John Gazette*, July 29, 1800.

CAUTION

Whereas some evil minded person, set on by the instigation of the Devil, has been on board of the SHIP I am now building near the Old Fort at CARLETON, and have maliciously or in a fit of insanity, cut the edges of the cieling plank, so that they are damaged thereby. I hereby Caution all persons whatsoever, on their peril, whether out of malice, madness, or otherwise to desist from the like practices in future as I am determined to prosecute the offender to the extremity of the Law.

ARCHIBALD GILLIES

St. John, 24th July, 1800

---

* Unless otherwise stated, the dimensions and tonnage of all vessels are taken from the vessel's first registration.

Eden and Gascoyne Rivers (detail)

From *The Atlantic Neptune*
by J. F. W. Des Barres.
Engraved by H. Ashby, 1779.

Courtesy of the Dalhousie
University Library, Halifax, N.S.
William Inglis Morse Collection.

The large vessel is a fine example of a merchant ship of the mid-eighteenth century. The large two-masted vessel on the right appears to be a topsail schooner, with square topsails on both fore and main masts. The other small two-masted vessels are probably shallops, a term applied to small schooners which were open or only half-decked.

The logbook of the Dart

Prizes and Privateers

In October 1749 the Court of Vice Admiralty was established in Halifax. While its main duty was to deal with prizes of war and vessels caught engaging in illegal trade, it also heard disputes over seamen's wages, salvage, marine contracts and damages to vessels and their cargoes.

Shortly after England's declaration of war with France in August 1756, the Vice Admiralty Court was authorized to issue a Letter of Marque to private ships of war. This document was in effect a licence to capture, by force if necessary, vessels, goods and merchandise belonging to the enemies of Great Britain. When a Letter of Marque was issued, details of the ship's armament, tonnage, etc., and the names of the owners, officers and men were registered with the Court of Vice Admiralty. A record of the proceedings on board the privateer and a list of vessels captured had to be kept. Ships seized by privateers were taken to the nearest Vice Admiralty Court, condemned as prizes and then sold at public auction. The captor received as much as one-third to one-half the amount obtained. There was, in fact, keen competition between the privateers and ships of the Royal Navy in this lucrative enterprise.

In July 1756, even before war had been declared, William Knox fitted out the sloop *Sea Flower* and petitioned Governor Lawrence for a Letter of Marque. The petition was granted and Knox sailed eastward, hoping to capture French vessels engaging in illegal trade with Cape Breton.

From November 16, 1756, to June 20, 1760, official records indicate that Letters of Marque were issued to sixteen vessels. The first of these was the *Lawrence*, a schooner of 100 tons owned by Malachy Salter and Robert Saunderson of Halifax.

For several months before war was officially declared between Great Britain and the New England colonies, American privateers had been intercepting British shipping and several raids had been made along the Nova Scotia coast. By the end of 1776 nearly 350 prizes had been captured by American vessels.[1] In December of that year, the Nova Scotia Government fitted out an armed schooner of 50 tons with the rather appropriate name of *Loyal Nova Scotian*. Many other privateers were issued Letters of Marque and many prizes were taken. The losses to British and Colonial shipping were also very high. Unfortunately, since many of the records of the Vice Admiralty Court in Halifax as well as many of the shipping registers for this period are missing, it is impossible to determine how many vessels were captured by Maritime privateers.

An important contemporary source of information on the business of privateering is the diary of Simeon Perkins. The diary, which runs from 1766 until Perkins's death in 1812, gives a detailed and fascinating account of the involvement of the Liverpool and Halifax merchants in privateering enterprises, as well as details of the losses to Maritime shipping.

The renewal of the war with France in 1793 resulted in yet another period of privateering activity and more prizes were captured from the French and the Spanish. However, by 1798 Great Britain faced a serious problem from losses in merchant shipping. In 1807 Britain was effectively cut off from timber supplies from the Baltic and was forced to turn to the North American Colonies for ships and timber. This led to the first great shipbuilding period in the Maritimes.

The declaration of war on Great Britain by the United States in June 1812 resulted in the last and most active period of privateering. Between July 17, 1812, and January 24, 1815, the Court of Vice Admiralty records list thirty-one vessels which were issued with Letters of Marque. Most of these were owned by merchants in Halifax and Liverpool as well as in Saint John, St. Andrews and Annapolis Royal.

The *Liverpool Packet*, certainly one of the most famous of all the Nova Scotia privateers, was a schooner of 67 tons. Captured from the Spanish and condemned as a prize, she was registered at Halifax in 1811. Owned by Enos Collins of Halifax and Benjamin Knaut and John and James Barss of Liverpool, the vessel was granted a Letter of Marque on August 24, 1812. The schooner was armed with five guns and carried a crew of 45 men. The master on the first voyage was John Freeman and on the second, Joseph Barss.

On June 9, 1813, the *Liverpool Packet* was captured by the American privateer *Thomas*, taken into Portsmouth, renamed *Portsmouth Packet* and became an American privateer. Later in October she was recaptured by H.M. Brig *Fantome*, brought into Halifax, condemned in the Court of Vice Admiralty and registered at Halifax on November 22. The vessel, now owned by Enos Collins and Joseph Allison of Halifax, Joseph Freeman of Liverpool and the master, Caleb Seely of Saint John, once again renewed her privateering activities. In all, the *Liverpool Packet* captured approximately fifty vessels and certainly made a fortune for her owners. The American privateer *Thomas*, which had captured the *Liverpool Packet*, was herself captured by the British, condemned and sold in Halifax and became the schooner *Wolverine*, another Liverpool privateer.

Advertisements listing prize vessels for sale at Halifax and Liverpool regularly appeared in the Halifax paper. The market was swamped and the number of new vessels built fell dramatically. In 1813, of the 172 new registrations at Halifax 159 were prizes. During the same year, 32 prize vessels were placed on the Saint John register and only 12 new vessels were built. As the number of prizes fell during the next two years, the number of new vessels built steadily increased. Other Maritime registry ports were relatively unaffected by prizes. Only a few were registered at Shelburne, two at Sydney and none in Prince Edward Island.

From 1812 to 1815 over 440 vessels, captured by privateers and Royal Navy ships and designated as prizes, were added to the registry books in the Maritime Provinces. Many Maritime vessels were in turn captured or destroyed by the French and Americans. A number were captured and recaptured several times.

The Privateer SCHOONER
Liverpool.
George Young Commander.

Mounts Eight Carriage Guns with Swivels and small Arms.

All British Seamen and others willing to engage in the above Vessel, bound on a Cruize to the Southward for four Months and to return to this Port will meet with every encouragement and have a protection from the Press, by applying to Capt. Young at Mr. White's Tavern at the Slip.

No Person belonging to the Navy or Army will be taken, and to prevent Deserters from imposing themselves by false pretences, it is requested that their officers will apply to James Greenlow at Mr. Proud's, opposite the Market House and they shall be shewn every person engaged in the above Privateer.

Courtesy of the Legislative Library, Halifax, N.S.

Notices urging men to join the privateers appeared regularly in the Halifax papers. These were printed in the *Nova Scotia Gazette* on January 12, 1779. Men belonging to His Majesty's Navy or Army were not eligible to join as crew.

Revenge Privateer.
Commanded by Capt *James Gandy,*
Who has been on several Cruizes, and met with great Success.

All Gentlemen Volunteers; Seamen, and able bodied Landsmen, who wish to acquire Riches and Honor, are invited to repair on board the *Revenge* Privateer ship of War, now laying in *Halifax* Harbour; mounting Thirty Carriage Guns, with Cohorns, wivels, &c. bound on a Cruize to the Southward for four Months against the French, and all His Majesty's Enemies, and then to return to this Harbour.

All Volunteers will be received on board the said ship—or by Captain *James Gandy,* at his Rendezvous at Mr. *Proud's* Tavern near the Market House, where they will meet with all due Encouragement, and the best Treatment; Proper Advance will be given.

GOD save the KING.

N. B. As it is expected that many of the Loyal Inhabitants of this Province, will try their Fortunes by entering on board so good a ship and at such a favorable Time, a Protection will be given to prevent their being impressed on board Men of War——As no Time is to be lost, the ship will go to sea in Fourteen Days, great Part so the Crew being engaged.

If any Men belonging to His Majesty's Navy, or Army, should attempt under any Disguise or Pretence whatsoever to offer themselves they may depend on being secured, and prosecuted.

The Rover

One of the most famous of the Liverpool privateers at the turn of the century was the *Rover*, a brig of 100 tons built at Liverpool in 1800. The vessel was owned by Joseph Freeman and a number of Liverpool merchants including Simeon Perkins. In September 1800 the vessel gained fame after she captured the Spanish schooner *Santa Rita*. An account of the capture was printed in the Naval Chronicle in 1801.

Our Readers should be informed, that the Royal Province of NOVA SCOTIA, (America) having suffered most severely in the early part of the War, from the Cruises of the Enemy, fitted out a number of Privateers, in order to retaliate on, and to extort compensation from, the Foe. Within these four years, twelve or fifteen private Ships of War have been fitted out by the Nova Scotians, and of this number one half are owned by the little Village of Liverpool, which boasts the honour of having launched the Brig Rover, the Hero of our present relation.

We have been favoured with the following extract of a Letter, dated Liverpool, October 17, from Captain GODFREY, of the armed Brig ROVER, which contains a very modest relation of a gallant Action, that reflects the highest honour on Captain Godfrey and the brave Men under his Command:

"The Brig Rover, mounting 14 four-pounders, was the present year built and fitted for War at Liverpool in this Province; she sailed under my Command the 4th of June last on a Cruise against the Enemies of Great Britain, being Commissioned by his Excellency Sir John Wentworth, Bart. Our Crew consisted of 55 Men and Boys, including myself and Officers, and was principally composed of Fishermen. . . . On the 10th of September, being cruising near to Cape Blanco, on the Spanish Main, we chased a Spanish Schooner on shore and destroyed her. Being close in with the Land and becalmed, we discovered a Schooner and three Gun-boats under Spanish Colours making for us; a light breeze springing up, we were enabled to get clear of the Land, when it fell calm, which enabled the Schooner and Gun-boats, by the help of a number of oars, to gain fast upon us, keeping up at the same time a constant fire from their bow guns, which we returned with two guns pointed from our stern; one of the Gun-boats did not advance to attack us. As the enemy drew near we engaged them with muskets and pistols, keeping with oars the stern of the Rover towards them, and having all our guns well loaded with great and small shot, ready against we should come to close quarters. When we heard the Commander of the Schooner give orders to the two Gun-boats to board us, I waited to see how they meant to attack us, and finding the Schooner intended to board us on our starboard quarter, one of the Gun-Boats on our larboard bow, and the other on our larboard waist, I suffered them to advance in that position until they came within about fifteen yards, still firing on them with small arms and the stern guns; I then manned the oars on the larboard side, and pulled the Rover round so as to bring her starboard broadside to bear athwart the Schooner's bow, and poured into her a whole broadside of great and small shot, which raked her deck fore and aft, while it was full of Men ready for boarding. I instantly shifted over to the other side and raked both Gun-boats in the same manner, which must have killed and wounded a great number of those on board of them, and done great damage to their Boats. I then comenced a close Action with the Schooner, which lasted three glasses, and having disabled her sails and rigging much, and finding her fire grow slack, I took advantage of a light air of Wind to back my head sails, which brought my stern on board of the Schooner, by which we were enabled to board her and carry her, at which time the Gun-boats sheered off, apparently in a very shattered condition. We found her to be the Santa Ritta [sic], mounting ten six pounders and two twelve pound carronades, with 125 Men. She was fitted out the day before, by the Governor of Porto Cavallo, with the Gun-boats, for the express purpose of taking us; every officer on board of her was killed except the Officers who commanded a party of twenty-five Soldiers; there were fourteen men dead on her deck when we boarded her, and seventeen wounded; the Prisoners, including the wounded, amounted to seventy-one. My Ship's Company, including Officers and Boys, was only 45 in number, and behaved with that courage and spirit which British Seamen always show when fighting the Enemies of their Country. It is with infinite pleasure I add, that I had not a Man hurt. . . ."

The *Rover* continued as a privateer. Captain Godfrey was offered a commission in the Royal Navy but refused the honour. He entered into the West Indies trade and in 1803, died of yellow fever and was buried at Kingston, Jamaica.

The photograph on the right is a page from the records of the Court of Vice Admiralty in Halifax and shows the entries for the *Nostra Seignora del Carmen* and the *Santa Rita*, two schooners captured by the *Rover*.

Cause 5 1800

Nova Scotia
Court of Vice
Admiralty } The Attorney General for and in behalf as well of His Majesty as Alexander Godfrey Master of the Privateer Rover being a Brig fitted out as a Private Vessel of War under the Authority of Government, and the Owners Officers and Crew of said Vessel. ——

Versus —

The Schooner Nostra Seignora del Carmen

17th October 1800 } Libel filed and entered, Order made thereon as on file ——

7th November 1800 } Court opened by making Proclamation as usual — Decree pronounced as on file. ——

Cause 6 1800

Nova Scotia
Court of Vice
Admiralty } The Attorney General for and in behalf as well of His Majesty as Alexander Godfrey Master of the Privateer Rover being a Brig fitted out as a private Vessel of War under the Authority of Government and the Owners, Officers and Crew of said Vessel. ——

Versus —

The Schooner Santa Rita & Cargo

17th October 1800 } Libel filed and entered, Order made thereon as on file

11th November 1800 } Court opened by making Proclamation as usual — Decree pronounced as on file. ——

Court of Vice Admiralty Record.

Courtesy of the Public Archives of Nova Scotia, Halifax, N.S.

The Dart

On May 22, 1813, the sloop *Dart*, armed with four six-pounders and carrying a crew of twenty-five men, left Saint John on a privateering cruise. The vessel was itself a prize, captured from the Americans, condemned in the Court of Vice Admiralty in Halifax on March 10, 1813, and sold for the sum of £535. She was registered at Saint John on May 4, 1813, and owned by Robert Shivers, James Hay Jr. and James T. Hanford, merchants of Saint John. A Letter of Marque was issued on May 7, 1813, by the Court of Vice Admiralty in Halifax. The *Dart* was one of four privateers operating out of Saint John during the period of the War of 1812.

The following excerpts are taken from a journal kept by the Master, John Harris.

St. John, N.B. May 22nd, 1813
> Moderate breeze and pleasant weather at Noon mustered the men by the custom house Office — at 1 P.M. got underweigh and dropt down to the beacon and came to with the Best bower All hands employed getting the vessel ready for sea Wind W S W. . . .

Monday May 24th
> 2 p.m. got underweigh and proceeded out of the Harbour on a cruise. . . .

Tuesday, May 25th
> . . . all hands employed in making wads, points and getting the guns and small arms in order. . . .

Friday, 28th
> Light airs inclinable to calm at 4 P.M. saw a schooner making into little river at 6 P.M. sent Mr Ross 1st Leut and six men in the boat to bring her out at 10 the boat returned had boarded her she proved to be the Sally of and from Eastport bound to Machias having a Licence and in Ballast
> At ½ past 2 A.M. being dark thick weather fell in with his Majesty Ship Rattler Capt Gordon. She fired two Shots at us in Quick succession one of which came into our Larboard Bow between wind and water — came to Anchor immediately and Rattlers boat boarded me went on board the Rattler. Capt Gordon sent his Cappenter Who plug'd and leaded the hole. at 4 Returned on board and continued on our Cruise. . . .

Monday, May 31st 1813
> . . . 11 [A.M.] Saw three sail in shore stand'g to the east^d — Gave chase immediately. . . .

Wednesday, June 2nd 1813
> . . . at 4 PM too & Boarded and captured Schooner Joanna Capt Newcomb from Boston Bound to East port laded with fifteen hundred bushels corn pr Clearance, put Nathaniel Ricker prize master and three hands on board and ordered her for St. Johns, N.B. Allowed the Master to go on Shore in his Boat he wished to continue in the prize but had made use of such threatning language that it was thought prudent to send him on Shore. . . .

Friday, June 4th 1813
> . . . 10 [AM] Inclinable to Calm — Saw a Large Ship to the S west^d of Cape Ann A Fishing Boat spoke us and cautioned us from going round the lights saying the Ship we saw was and English frigate and that the Chesepeake Frigate was Chased in or taken by the Shannon — could not assertain which not wishing him to come near us. . . .

Saturday, June 5th, 1813
> . . . 8 PM stood toward the shore intending to try to cut out the Pilot Boat schooner in Sandy Bay. Midnight moderate Breeze and hazy close in with halibut point
> Out Boat and mand her with 7 men under the command of Mr Owen 2nd Leiut, armd with one swivel, small arms, cutlases and pistols and ordered her into sandy bay to bring out the aforesaid schooner.
> 2 AM Calm and hazy lying between the Salvages and sandy bay.
> 3 AM the boat returned & reported had examined the Bay and that the schooner had Escaped. In Boat and mand the sweeps and rowed out past thatcher Lights 5 in sweeps and made sail having a light breeze from the southward — Saw a schooner to the westward Standing to the eastward.
> 6 AM almost calm, being about 3 miles from the schooner sent Mr Ross with the Boat to board her.
> 7 [AM] got sight of the pilot Boat schooner working along shore near Gloster Point.
> 8 Mr Ross returned the schooner was the Mary of Dorchester Capt. Wilson from Boston for Portland being light and an old vessel allowed her to proceed — Housed our guns and kept all hands below, least the schooner should suspect us and Escape into A harbour.
> 11 coming up with the chase. at 11½ AM brought her too,

being off Salem Harbour near the Half way rock — sent Mr Ross and Boats Crew on board ordered him to make sail out of the Bay immediately — While I boarded and took in tow the Chebauo Boat — and Stood out again — the Boat was called ye Superb of Portland Lemuel Sawyer Master Cargo Salt and the Schooner proved to be the Washington of Portland from & for Boston Elisha Sawyer, Master and owner — Cargo of Lumber — a Beautiful Pilot Boat of 65 tons burden entirely new, pierced for Guns, completely fitted and I expect was intended for a privateer. . . .

Sunday, June 6th, 1813

. . . 3½ PM sent Willm Owen 2nd Leiut and two men on board the Washington and Ordered Her for St John, N.B. having previously put on board 1 swivel two muskets two Cutlass and Sixty Rounds — She being so fine a Vessell and having a warlike appearance judged proper to arm her likewise put on board provisions & c. . . .²

The *Dart* continued on her cruise and during the next three weeks captured three more prizes. She returned to Saint John on July 1, and John Harris left the vessel and returned to Annapolis Royal.

A second Letter of Marque was issued to the *Dart* on July 15. The new master was James Ross, possibly the "Mr. Ross, 1st Leut." [sic] referred to in the journal. During the next two months the *Dart* captured six more prizes, all of which were condemned in the Court of Vice Admiralty in Halifax. The fate of the *Dart* is not known. The copy of the Register is not cancelled. She does not appear to have been sold and transferred to another port, but may have suffered the fate of many vessels during this period and been captured by the Americans.

The Early Nineteenth Century

The first sharp increase in shipbuilding in the Maritimes occurred during the first two decades of the nineteenth century. Although shipbuilding declined owing to the increase in the number of prizes in 1813 and 1814, by 1816 the number of new vessels had risen to 250. The area most affected by the presence of prizes was, of course, the mainland of Nova Scotia. In 1813 only twelve new vessels were built. From that date, however, as the number of prizes fell, shipbuilding quickly increased, especially in Pictou, Yarmouth, Liverpool and Cornwallis township.

Halifax was rapidly becoming a major port and a number of merchants became established in the city, as a result of the War of 1812. The most prominent of these were Joseph Allison, Enos Collins, William Pryor and Samuel Cunard. Cunard began in 1813 with the purchase of a number of prizes which he operated in the West Indies trade. Within a few years he was not only operating his own vessels but having vessels built for sale in England. It was the start of an enterprise that was to become the Cunard Steamship Company.

Saint John was less affected than Halifax by the increase in prizes. New Brunswick continued to lead in the size of vessels built. Between 1811 and 1813, seven large ships of over 400 tons were built in New Brunswick and registered in Saint John. The number of vessels being built for immediate transfer to the British Isles was steadily increasing as more agents for British companies were being established. In 1799 Christopher Scott had arrived in Saint John to superintend the building of vessels for his brothers in Greenock, Scotland. Other Saint John merchants included John Ward, William Lawson, Ezekiel Barlow, Thomas Millidge and William Pagan, all major ship owners.

Shipbuilding in Prince Edward Island increased steadily as more vessels were built for British owners. Others were being sold in Newfoundland. The first three-masted schooner built in the Maritimes of which we have records was the *Dispatch* of 128 tons, constructed in Murray River, Prince Edward Island, in 1814. The vessel was owned by Lemuel and John Cambridge and registered in Prince Edward Island until 1823, when she was transferred to Bristol, England and owned by John Cambridge.

In 1817 the *Malvina*, of 129 tons, another three-masted schooner, was built in Bedeque and owned by Samuel Welsford. The following year the vessel was transferred to Liverpool, England and owned by John Green.

In 1815, Lemuel and John Cambridge built the *Mary*, a ship of 374 tons, the largest vessel to be built on the Island up to that time. In 1822 the *Mary*, now rigged as a barque but still owned by the Cambridge company, was registered at Bristol.

Sloop

This illustration shows a typical sloop of the early nineteenth century, a rig common around the coast. The vessel carries a gaff mainsail and three headsails which are furled. The yards on the mainmast and topmast are for setting a square mainsail and topsail when running before the wind. The gaff mainsail is loose-footed and the tack has been triced up to spill the wind.

Sloop

Detail: St Mary's River.
Sepia wash drawing
by John Woolford, c. 1818.

Courtesy of the Dalhousie
University Library, Halifax, N.S.
William Inglis Morse Collection.

Trade and Timber 1820-1845

The period from 1820 to 1845 saw the first great increase in shipping and shipbuilding and is perhaps one of the most interesting in the history of the Maritimes. The shipping registers are complete, and after 1824 the names of the shipbuilders are usually included in the register. An increasing number of newspapers were being published, providing information on launchings, sailings and cargoes. A large number of shipbuilders, agents and companies who were to dominate the scene for many years were established during this period.

During the Napoleonic Wars, the duty on timber imported to Britain from Europe had been very high while colonial timber was imported almost duty-free. The result had been a rapid increase in the imports of colonial timber to the United Kingdom. Although the duty on foreign timber was reduced in 1821 from £3–5–0 to £2–5–0 per load and a duty of 10 shillings per load imposed on colonial timber, the North American colonies were still left at a tremendous advantage. The recovery from the post-war depression saw an increase in timber prices, freight rates and wages and a sudden demand for Canadian timber and Canadian vessels.[1]

The result was an enormous increase in shipbuilding and timber exports, especially in New Brunswick. St. Andrews was opened as a port of registry in 1823, Miramichi in 1826. Shipbuilding was also becoming a major industry throughout Nova Scotia. After

Shelburne closed as a port of registry in 1823, Halifax and Sydney remained as the two ports of registry until Pictou, Yarmouth and Liverpool were opened in 1840 and Arichat in 1842. Prince Edward Island also saw a rapid increase in shipbuilding, and a greater number of the vessels being built were sent to England.

A change was made in the format of the shipping register in 1824. The number of shares held by each person was now indicated, as well as the name of the builder. As the shares of vessels were bought and sold, endorsements were often made on the vessel's register to indicate the change of ownership. In many cases, however, the vessel was simply given a new registration. This practice had, in fact, been in effect since 1787. However, as shipbuilding increased and many people became involved in the ownership of vessels, the system became very cumbersome. Many vessels were re-registered several times in one year.

The list of new registrations for a particular port in any one year will, therefore, contain not only the names of vessels being registered for the first time, but also the names of vessels being re-registered. In 1839, for example, 186 new registrations were added to the Saint John register. Of these, 101 were newly built vessels while the remaining 85 were re-registrations. A look at the number of new registrations at a port for a particular year may, therefore, give a very false picture of shipbuilding activity. This practice of constant re-registration was continued until the new Navigation

Act of 1854, when the transaction system was put into effect.

Before 1824 records had quickly become inaccurate because many of the registers were not cancelled when the vessels passed out of existence or were transferred to other ports. The new Act of 1823 required that all vessels still in existence be registered. It is clear also that before 1824 many small vessels were not registered at all. Many of these, some of which were several years old, now appeared on the register for the first time. The result is a more accurate picture of how many vessels were being built per year and of how many still remained on the registry books at any one time. There was a general tightening-up of regulations and the introduction of new ones to ensure a greater control by the authorities.

Also, after 1824 an increasing number of vessels were sent to England on a Governor's Pass. This was a certificate allowing the vessel to proceed directly to Britain to be registered without first being registered at a Canadian port.

This era saw an improvement in the number of aids to navigation, such as the establishment of markers, buoys and lighthouses. As early as 1758 a lighthouse had been built at Sambro, at the mouth of Halifax Harbour, and another one was built on Partridge Island at the entrance to Saint John Harbour in 1791. However, it was not until the early nineteenth century that any number were built along the coast.

As early as 1801, a gun had been placed on Partridge Island to be used in fog, but it was later replaced by an enormous bell. Neither was very successful and numerous other methods were tried. In 1854 Robert Foulis developed the world's first foghorn at Saint John. It was operated by steam and first installed on Partridge Island in 1859.

An important stimulus to the major business communities in the Maritimes was the establishment of a number of banks during the early nineteenth century. In 1801 efforts had been made to establish a bank in Halifax and £50,000 was subscribed. However, the demand of the company for a monopoly resulted in the bill being deferred by the House of Assembly. Further unsuccessful attempts were made in 1811, 1822 and 1825.

The first chartered bank in Canada was the Bank of New Brunswick, established in 1820. The names of John Robinson, William Black, Thomas Millidge, Nehemiah Merritt, Robert Pagan, Christopher Scott, William Botsford and Ward Chipman Jr. were included in the list of shareholders.

On September 3, 1825, the Halifax Banking Company was established as a private enterprise in Halifax. The eight shareholders included Henry H. Cogswell, William Pryor, Enos Collins, James Tobin, Samuel Cunard and Joseph Allison. The company had no charter or Act of Incorporation but soon became very successful. Five of the shareholders were members of the Executive and Legislative Councils. However, their autocratic behaviour soon resulted in a number of strong attacks and within a few years other merchants were advocating the establishment of a public bank.

The initial meeting took place on January 4, 1832, and shortly afterwards the Bill of Incorporation was introduced in the Legislature by William Lawson. Despite strong opposition, the Bill was passed in late March and the Bank of Nova Scotia came into being.

The 1820s saw an increase in the number of watercolours and oils of vessels built in the Maritimes. Many of these contain the name of the vessel and are dated, thus making positive identification possible. A large number of original sketches and engravings are extant. Scenes by Pooley, Woolford, Eagar, Hickman, Bartlett and many others often show the types of vessels found along the coast and give interesting details on rigging. Magazines such as the *Illustrated London News*, which first appeared in 1842, are also valuable sources of information.

The Tantivy

In the Saint John area a number of builders were established during the 1820s. John Owens began building at Portland in 1821 and over the next eleven years launched thirty vessels. In 1825 he built the *Saint George* of 204 tons, the first steamer to be registered at Saint John. In 1833 he was joined by John Duncan, a partnership that was to continue for twenty years. Most of their vessels were large ships and barques of 400 to 1000 tons, intended for British owners. In 1847 they built the *Forest Monarch*, a ship of 1542 tons which they owned themselves until she was lost two years later.

By 1824 John Haws had established his yard at Portland and continued building for thirty-two years. Some years after his death in 1858, the Haws yard was sold to Thomas Hilyard.

Between 1823 and 1828 George Thompson built a number of vessels at L'Etang, Sackville and Hillsborough before moving to Portland in 1829. From then until 1841 he built another twenty-six vessels. Nearly all were ships and barques of 500 to 1000 tons destined for sale in Great Britain.

A number of shipyards had also been established on the Saint John and Kennebecasis Rivers. Justus S. Wetmore had begun building at Kingston as early as 1822 and possibly before. From then until 1847, thirty-seven vessels were launched. These included ships, barques, brigs, schooners and steamers. In 1845 he launched the *Robert Rankin*, a three-masted schooner of 255 tons. Benjamin Appleby built his first vessel, the *Elizabeth*, a small brig of 127 tons, at Hampton in 1832 and continued building for another twenty years.

One of the most popular rigs of the early nineteenth century was the brig, a vessel with two masts, both square-rigged. In 1825, a peak year for shipbuilding in Saint John, forty-five of the 140 new vessels were brigs, ranging in size from 127 to 394 tons. Thirty-six of these were sold in England within a year.

The *Tantivy*, a brig of 313 tons, was built by Samuel Huston at Norton and launched on October 24, 1827. The vessel was owned by Thomas Hanford and Thomas Raymond, merchants of Saint John, and remained on the Saint John register until lost on Sable Island on November 21, 1834.

The *Tantivy* is shown in this painting under full sail with the wind fine on the port quarter. She carries courses, topsails, topgallants and royals. The skysails are being clewed up. She also carries topsail, topgallant and royal studdingsails on both the fore and main masts on the port side. The fore studdingsail is being taken in. As was common in many paintings of this period, a stern view of the brig is shown on the right.

The Tantivy

Brig   313 Tons
Built in 1827 at Norton, N.B.,
by Samuel Huston.
103'4" x 26'3"

Oil on canvas.
Unsigned and undated.
Courtesy of the New Brunswick
Museum, Saint John, N.B.

The Jessie

On September 13, 1818, the brigantine *Peter & Sarah* of Bideford, England, entered Charlottetown. On board were John Eastridge, master mariner, William Ellis, shipwright, and a crew of six or seven men. In the hold were clothing, supplies, equipment and tools, ironwork and rope to build, equip and rig a small sailing ship. The owner of the brigantine was Thomas Burnard, a merchant of Bideford, and the voyage marked the beginning of an enterprise which was to exploit the timber possibilities of Prince Edward Island and to develop a major shipbuilding industry.

The *Peter & Sarah* proceeded to Lot 12, Richmond Bay. Land was cleared for a small settlement (to be called New Bideford) and accommodations built for the winter. By late fall the *Peter & Sarah* had returned to Bideford, England, and William Ellis and his men began cutting timber for the new vessel. In the spring, Thomas Burnard Chanter, nephew of Burnard, arrived to manage his uncles affairs in the new enterprise.

The new vessel, the *Mars*, a ship of 341 tons, was launched in the late fall and registered at Prince Edward Island on November 8, 1819. The registered owner was William Ellis, agent for Thomas Burnard, and the vessel sailed for Bideford, England, loaded with a cargo of timber.

William Ellis continued to build for Burnard with equipment, sails and rigging sent from England, and Thomas Chanter served as agent until Burnard's sudden death in 1823. Two years later the operation was taken over by Thomas Chanter, who soon afterwards sold out to William Ellis. The heir of Thomas Burnard, however, was to be James Yeo, an immigrant from North Cornwall, whom Burnard had brought over from England some years before to superintend the timber operations. Within the next few years, Yeo took over the enterprise and developed one of the largest shipbuilding and exporting operations in Prince Edward Island. William Ellis continued his shipbuilding activity and eventually became master builder for James Yeo. In 1853 he built his last and his largest vessel for Yeo, the *Princess Royal*, a ship of 905 tons.

William Ellis and Thomas Chanter were not the only ones to take advantage of the great timber possibilities of Prince Edward Island, and the early 1820s saw a rapid increase in the number of vessels built in the Island and sent to England. One of the early merchants was John Cambridge, a British Quaker who had come from Bristol in 1784 as an agent for Robert Clark. After Clark's failure, Cambridge remained and soon became a prominent shipbuilder and merchant. After his death in 1831, the business was continued by his sons, Lemuel at Murray River and Artemas in Bristol, England. Their names appear regularly on the Island shipping registers until the late 1840s.

The *Jessie*, a brig of 135 tons, was built by William Ellis at New Bideford in 1827. The vessel was registered in Prince Edward Island and owned by Thomas Chappell and Joshua Williams of Appledore, England. On March 4, 1838, she was registered at Bideford, England, and traded out of that port for many years.

This watercolour of the *Jessie* shows the rigging of a brig from the weather side. She carries courses, topsails, topgallants and a royal on the main. The house flag, "J.W.," is probably that of Joshua Williams, one of her owners at Bideford.

Brig JESSIE of BIDEFORD . PHILIP . LAWTON . MASTER .

The Jessie

Brig   135 Tons
Built in 1827 at New Bideford, P.E.I.
by William Ellis.
70'5" x 21'3" x 12'3"

Watercolour.
Unsigned and undated.
Courtesy of Mr. Basil Greenhill,
London and Parkhouse, Appledore.

The James

During the late 1820s Samuel Cunard was quickly expanding his ship-owning activities and was having vessels built in various parts of Nova Scotia and Cape Breton as well as in New Brunswick and Prince Edward Island. Two of the first of these were launched in Pictou in 1826: the *Jessie*, a brig of 345 tons built by Alexander MacKay, and the *Sir Walter Scott*, a brig of 218 tons, built by James Dawson. Other Nova Scotia builders included David Crichton, also of Pictou; William Douglas of Truro; and Isaac W. Doane of Sissiboo. After 1833 a large number of Cunard's vessels were built in Dartmouth by Alexander Lyle. Two of the largest of these were the *Lady Lilford*, a ship of 596 tons, built in 1838 and the *Nereid*, a barque of 672 tons, built in 1841.

Several of the first large vessels built in Cape Breton were owned by Samuel Cunard. In 1826 at Bras d'Or Lake, James Cain launched the *John Bainbridge*, a barque of 365 tons, and, in the following year, the *Samuel Cunard*, a ship of 303 tons.

While shipbuilding in Cape Breton continued to be very active, it was mainly confined to small craft. Nearly all were locally owned. Most of the shipbuilding was centred around Sydney, Arichat, Little Arichat, Cheticamp, Baddeck, Harbour Bouche and Ship Harbour. Arichat opened as a port of registry in 1842. Peak years occurred in 1826, with 32 vessels and in 1840, with 40 vessels. In 1831, J. M. Moffett built the *Sibella*, a three-masted schooner of 101 tons at Sydney.

The *James*, a brig of 213 tons, was built in 1826 by Peter Brouard at Ship Harbour (now Port Hawkesbury), and owned by the builder and Thoum, Moulin & Company of Guernsey. The vessel was registered at Syndney in 1826 and subsequently registered at Guernsey.

This watercolour of the *James* is one of the earliest illustrations of a named Maritime-built vessel. The detail is especially fine. She is shown under full sail off Trieste and wears the Moulin house flag at the main truck. The small sails shown on the weather side of the topsails and topgallants are studdingsails. These were supplementary sails used in light winds.

The *James* is technically a "snow": a special type of brig that carried her spanker on a separate trysail mast abaft the mainmast. A distinction between brig and snow is not always made in the shipping registers. The term "snow" does occur occasionally in the late eighteenth and early nineteenth century Canadian shipping registers, but more often the rig is described as a brig with a trysail mast.

The James

Brig   213 Tons
Built in 1826 at Ship Harbour, N.S.,
by Peter John Brouard.

Watercolour.
Painted by F. Polli, Trieste, 1828.
Courtesy of the Nova Scotia
Museum, Halifax, N.S.

The Albion

William Olive was another of the early shipbuilders of Saint John. Like many others, his was a family business, and two of his brothers, Isaac and James, helped in the yard. The names of William Jr. and Isaac Olive appear in 1818 as the owners of the *Brothers*, a schooner of 66 tons which they probably built. Five years later, they built at Carleton the *Caledonia*, a ship of 410 tons. For more than forty years they launched at least one, and often two, large vessels each year. While many were built for sale in England, others were locally owned. When William retired the yard was taken over by his sons, who continued building until the mid-1870s.

On November 18, 1834, William and Isaac Olive launched the *Albion*, a ship of 687 tons. Four days later the *New Brunswick Courier* reported:

Launches: On Tuesday last, about 1 o'clock, was launched from the Ship Yard of Messrs. I & W Olive, Carleton, the Ship ALBION of 700 tons owned by Mr. John Hammond of this city. This superior and splendid vessel has been only four months in building. She is to be commanded by Capt. T. Mowatt.

The vessel was registered at Saint John and owned by John Hammond for thirteen years. She was sold and registered at Liverpool, England, on January 5, 1848.

This view of the *Albion*, taken from the weather side, shows the vessel under full sail and gives a wealth of rigging detail. The positions of the standing and running rigging are clearly shown. The ship carries courses, topsails, topgallants and royals, and wears the Hammond house flag on the fore truck. The rows of reef bands and the reef points on the courses and on the topsails are clearly visible.

The reef bands were reinforcing strips of canvas stretching across the width of the sails; to these were attached short lengths of rope called reef points. When it became necessary to reduce sail, the ends of the reef bands were drawn up to the yard arm by means of tackles. The reef points were then passed up on either side of the yard and tied at the top. In this way the reef band became the head of the sail and the yard was lowered to accommodate the reduction in sail area. Large sails might have as many as three or four reef bands and further reduction in sail was accomplished by consecutively taking in one reef band after another. To "shake out" a reef the procedure was reversed.

The Albion

Ship   687 Tons
Built in 1834 at Carleton, N.B.,
by William and Isaac Olive.
137′4″ x 33′2″

Oil on canvas.
Unsigned and undated.
Courtesy of the New Brunswick
Museum, Saint John, N.B.

St. Andrews, New Brunswick

During the American Revolution William Pagan and his associates had moved from Falmouth to Fort George on the Penobscot River. However, when the boundary was finally settled, they discovered that they were still on the wrong side of the border and in September, 1784, the "Penobscot Association" moved to St. Andrews.

By 1788 William Pagan was actively engaged in shipbuilding and his business continued well into the nineteenth century. While he operated a number of these vessels himself, many of the larger ones, ships and barques of 200 to 400 tons, were sent for sale in England. Two of these were the *Harmony*, a ship of 256 tons built in 1789, and the *Sheddens*, a ship of 420 tons built in 1801. Pagan owned both of these vessels for several years and maintained part ownership in them after they were transferred to England. In 1812 William and Robert Pagan, together with Robert Sterling Ritchie, owned the *Sir John Sherbrook*, a brig of 187 tons. The vessel was issued a Letter of Marque on November 27, 1812, and became an active privateer until captured by the Americans two years later.

Prominent shipbuilders of Charlotte County in the 1830s and 1840s included Joshua Briggs, John N. M. Brewer, James Rait and Robert and John Townsend. Many of the larger vessels were being built for British owners. One of the largest of these was the *Lord Ashburton*, a ship of 1009 tons launched by Briggs and Brewer at Brandy Cove in 1843. Vessels were also being built at St. Stephen, Deer Island, Grand Manan and Campobello. Two of the largest vessels launched in St. Stephen were the *Charles Humberston*, a ship of 640 tons built by Owen Hinds in 1838, and the *Schoodiac*, a ship of 1004 tons built by William Porter in 1844.

Shipbuilding declined in this area during the late 1850s as a result of the influx of American vessels. In 1863, out of thirty-seven new registrations at St. Andrews, thirty were American-built. Two of the best-known builders of the later years were Charles and John Short. Charles had apprenticed in the yard of Robert and John Townsend and later became master builder for John Wilson. In 1860 he was joined by his brother John, and the next year they began building at St. Stephen. During the next eighteen years they launched more than twenty vessels for Zachariah Chipman and John Bolton of St. Andrews and John S. DeWolf & Company of Liverpool, England. Their last vessel, and also their largest, was the *Rocklands*, a ship of 1465 tons launched in 1878 for Zachariah Chipman.

VIEW OF S? ANDREWS, N.B.

Miss A.D. Stevenson del? Robbinston, May 4?, 1834.

Lithograph.
Drawn by Miss A. D. Stevenson, 1834.

Courtesy of the New Brunswick
Museum, Saint John, N.B.

The St. George

Robert Ellis came to New Brunswick from Tynemouth, England, around 1800. In 1823 he established a shipyard at Tynemouth Creek and the next year launched his first vessel, the *Emulous*, a brig of 231 tons. From 1824 until 1837 Ellis built twenty-one vessels, nearly all of which were sold and registered in England. On June 28, 1836, he launched his largest vessel, the *St. George*, a ship of 665 tons.

The *New Brunswick Courier* published this report on July 16, 1836:

New Ship. Launched at Tynemouth, County of St. John, on the 28th ult. and was towed into this port by the steamer GAZELLE, on the 3ᵈ instant, the ship SAINT GEORGE, owned by Robert Ellis, Esquire under whose immediate superintendence she was constructed and is a substantial and well built vessel, and will carry a large cargo. Her masts and rigging have been put up since she was brought into port, and her loading was commenced on the 9th and it will probably be completed by the 16th inst., when, it is supposed her cargo of deals will admeasure about 500,000 superficial feet.

The *St. George* was registered at Saint John on July 4, 1836, and owned by Robert Ellis. She cleared Saint John on her maiden voyage on July 29 with a cargo of lumber bound for Newry, Ireland. In October, 1839, the vessel was registered at London, England.

Robert Ellis built one more vessel, the *England*, a ship of 484 tons, in 1837 before returning to England. The yard was then taken over by John S. Parker and Richard Lovett, two apprentices who had worked for Ellis and had married his two daughters, Bessie and Annie. In 1838 Parker and Lovett built two vessels, the *Will Watch*, a schooner of 47 tons, and the *Sarah Jane*, a brig of 206 tons. From 1840 to 1854 they launched ten large vessels, the two largest being the *Simonds*, a ship of 1202 tons and the *Magnolia*, a ship of 1191 tons, both built in 1854. Shortly afterwards the partnership was dissolved and each continued building on his own.

This drawing of the *St. George* has been copied from a painting in the New Brunswick Museum and shows clearly the rigging detail on an early nineteenth century ship. A prominent characteristic of vessels of this period is the high rake of the bowsprit and the far forward position of the foremast, necessitating the forestay terminating far out on the bowsprit. As designs improved in later years, the space between the stem head and the foremast increased and the forestay moved inboard to be secured at or near the stem head. To strengthen the head gear further, the bowsprit was eventually lowered to be secured to the foredeck, and the stem head and the line of the bowsprit followed the sheer line of the vessel.

The St. George

Ship   665 Tons
Built in 1836 at Tynemouth, N.B.,
by Robert Ellis.
125.5′ x 28.5′ x 21.7′

Original painting in the
New Brunswick Museum, Saint John, N.B.
Traced by Charles A. Armour
from a photograph.

Halifax

During the early nineteenth century Halifax rapidly expanded and became an important shipping and business centre. Apart from Cunard, one of the largest companies in the 1820s was Enos Collins & Company, a partnership of Enos Collins, William B. Fairbanks and Joseph C. Allison. Born in 1774 at Liverpool, Nova Scotia, Enos Collins made his initial fortune in privateering during the Napoleonic Wars and the War of 1812. He rapidly became one of the wealthiest and most prominent businessmen of Halifax and, in 1825, was one of the main investors in the Halifax Banking Company. He retired from active business in 1859 and died at Halifax on November 9, 1871. His fortune has been estimated at between six and nine million dollars.

By 1826, James G. A. Creighton and Thomas Ritchie Grassie had joined partnership in the firm of Creighton and Grassie. In the late 1850s Thomas Grassie retired to England and the company continued as James G. A. Creighton and Sons until 1877. Other Halifax merchants included Thomas A. S. DeWolf, John and John Leander Starr, William Lawson Sr., William Lawson Jr. and Robert Lawson, Benjamin Wier, William Pryor, George Mitchell, William Stairs, James and Michael Tobin and John Duffus.

Vessels were being built at Dartmouth for Halifax owners. In 1824 John Chappell built his first vessel, the *Sir James Kempt*, a brig of 108 tons, for Enos Collins and Joseph Allison. Thomas Lowden built the *Atlantic*, a ship of 331 tons, in 1825 and in the following year the *Halifax*, a ship of 340 tons, both for the Halifax Packet Company. In 1826 Robert Lowden built the *Pacific*, a ship of 402 tons, for the Halifax Whaling Co., a joint ownership of Samuel Cunard, Joseph Allison and Lawrence Hartshorn. This was Cunard's first venture into the whaling business which he continued until the voyage of the *Rose* in 1843-1846.

In 1839 Samuel Cunard won the contract to carry the Royal Mail across the Atlantic, and the British and North American Royal Mail Steam Packet Company was incorporated. On May 16, 1840, the Cunard steamship *Unicorn*, the first transatlantic steamer to call at Halifax, arrived from Liverpool after a passage of sixteen days. On July 4, the *Britannia*, the first of the new Cunard steamships to be put into the Atlantic service, left Liverpool, England, and arrived at Halifax twelve and a half days later. A new era in transatlantic transportation had begun and the death knell of the sailing ship was sounded.

Samuel Cunard gradually transferred his business to England, leaving his sons in Halifax. He was knighted in 1859 and died in England on April 28, 1865. In 1878 the British and North American Royal Mail Steam Packet Company became the Cunard Steamship Company.

The Nova Scotian

Most newspapers of the nineteenth century published extensive information on shipping. Arrivals and clearances, as well as reports on launchings, accidents at sea and shipwrecks were often covered in detail.

This column on "shipping intelligence" appeared in the *Nova Scotian* for October 13, 1842. It lists vessels which have arrived and cleared at the port of Halifax, Nova Scotia. The vessel's name, rig, master's name and cargo are all given. For vessels entering the harbour, the length of the voyage is also noted.

Under the title "Manchester House" an advertisement appears for merchandise just received by Joseph Bell from England. Just below, James Cochran has also advertised for sale "Tobacco and Onions" received from New York and Boston.

SHIPPING INTELLIGENCE.

PORT OF HALIFAX.

ARRIVED

THURSDAY—Schr John Wallace, Burin, 12 days, dry fish, &c.; ketch Hertford, Buteau, Quebec, 18 days, pork, &c; brigt Antelope, Zuill, Demerara, 31 days, to G. R. Frith & Co; barque Auld, Liverpool, G B, 32 days, general cargo to W. Stairs & Son; schrs Acadian, Forest, St Peters, N F, molasses; James William, Antigonish, salmon; Peggy, Cape Breton, fish; Seaflower, Seven Brothers, Victoria, Two Brothers, Mary, Trial, and New Commerce, Sydney, coal; Hopewell, Canso, fish; Magnet, Arichat, do.

FRIDAY—Schr Minerva, Ross, Quebec, 15 days, flour, pork, &c.

SATURDAY—Schrs Good Intent, Gaspe, dry fish; Rambler, Canso, mackarel; brig Britannia, Gould, Cadiz, 58 days, salt.

SUNDAY—Schrs Lucy, O'Brien, Bathurst, 6 days, salmon and shingles; Sally, Lahave, fish.

MONDAY—Schrs Star, Cape Negro, dry fish; Echo, Shelburne, salt.

TUESDAY—H. M. Ship Rover, Com Keeles, Tampico, Mexico, with specie for the Commissariat; mailboat Roseway, Berwick, Bermuda, 10 days; brigt Eliza, Coffin, Montego Bay, 30 days; schr Gem, Graham, Boston, 3 days, flour and produce.

WEDNESDAY—Brigt Splendid, Swaine, Montego Bay, 30 days; Am brig Acadian, Jones, Boston, 2½ days, flour, onions &c; brigt Golden Rule, Spencer, Baltimore, 10 days, flour, pork, &c; steamer Saxe Gotha, Vaughan, St John, N B, (via immediate ports), 50 hours. Returned from sea H. M. Ship Vnlage, and H. M. Brigt Griffin.

THURSDAY—Brigt C. W. E. R., Smith, Antigua, 17 days, ballast; brigs Fanny, Willis, Jamaica, 28 days, ballast; Ambassador, Arestroup, Jamaica.

CLEARED.

THURSDAY, 6th inst—Am schr Atlantic, Nickerson, Philadelphia, mackarel, salmon, &c; brigt Index, Coalfleet, Jamaica, pork, flour, fish; schr Elizabeth, Murphy, Placentia, flour. 7th, brig Albion, Leslie, Miramichi, herrings. 8th, schrs Margaret Ann, Bellong, Pictou, bread, tea, sugar, &c; Breeze, Banks, Bermuda, pork, flour, &c; Esperance, Pirot, Gaspe, flour, herrings, &c; brigt Flotilla, Strickland, Demerara, lumber, staves, &c. 11th, schrs Unity, Hall Miramichi, tobacco, molasses, sugar, &c; John Thomas, Brookman, Sydney, C B, cargo from Boston. 12th, schrs Elizabeth, Harding, P E Island, molasses, &c; John Wallace, Lewis, Placentia, ballast.

Notice!

A TEMPERANCE MEETING will be held at the Literary Society's Room, in Dalhousie College, on Monday Evening next, at 8 o'clock, when the Committee appointed at a former meeting for the purpose of drafting Rules for the government of the Society, will lay them before the Meeting. All Temperance persons who are favorable to the scheme of combining moral, literary and scientific principles with those of Temperance, are expected and invited to attend. Her & Post

Near the old Stand.

THE SUBSCRIBER respectfully informs his friends and the Public, that he has taken the corner at the head of Bauer's Wharf, lately occupied by Mr. M. Donavan, and will continue his business as an AUCTION & GENERAL AGENT, and solicits a continuance of their Patronage.

A. B. JENNINGS.

October 6.   2m

Valuable New Work.

THE HARMONICAN.—A collection of the best PSALM & HYMN TUNES, now used in the B. N. A. Colonies with a variety of others, selected from the most approved Authors, and a copious introduction to vocal music. Published by JAMES DAWSON, Pictou.

Sold wholesale by the Publisher, and C. H. Belcher, Halifax, and retailed by Booksellers and Agents thoughout Nova Scotia and P. E. Island.

October 13.   Rec 3w

W & J. MURDOCH

HAVE Received their IMPORTATIONS from Great Britain, for this Autumn.

Oct. 13, 1842.   Rec 6w.

Manchester House.

THE Subscriber has just received by the "Medora," "Eliza Leishman," and "California," and offers for Sale at very low prices for Cash,

Pilot Cloths, Beavers, Tweeds, Doeskins and Vestings; white, red and Indigo blue Warp; Blankets, Flannels, Baizes, Serges and Kerseys; white and grey Shirting; Prints, Ginghams and Cambrics; Orleans Cloths, Victoria Saxonies, Lustres, Listados and Parisiennes; plain and printed M. de Laines; Linge de Lisle for evening dresses; Chene Chusans, Fashionable Cloakings, Ebor and Caroline Plaids for Childrens' Dresses; Silk Fringes and Gimps, Watered and Damask Moreen, Carpets, Hearth Rugs, and a variety of other goods.

The remainder of his Fall Supply daily expected by the London, and Prince George, from London.

JOSEPH BELL.

October 13.   4w

Tobacco, Onions, &c.

RECEIVED ex schr. Van Buren from New York, and schrs. John Thomas and Elizabeth from Boston.

390 kegs, boxes and half boxes Manufactured Tobacco mostly of the best Richmond brands,
300 barrels Onions, in prime order for shipping,
20 casks New York CHEESE,
9 boxes Looking Glasses, assorted
Boxes Hats, for covering,
Tierces Rice, casks Saleratus, bales Feathers,
Bales Quills, boxes Boots and Shoes, bags Coffee,
Sole Leather, boxes India Rubber Shoes,
Corn Brooms, Water Buckets,
Segars, Side Combs, &c. &c.

JAMES COCHRAN,

October 13.   Reg. & Jour. 4w   Water Street.

UNDER THE IMMEDIATE PATRONAGE OF

HER MAJESTY THE QUEEN:

THE PLAN

OF THE

NAVAL AND MILITARY OPERATIONS BEFORE QUEBEC

AND

DEATH OF WOLFE;

BY ALFRED HAWKINS,

Author of "The History of Quebec," &c.

Splendidly Engraved on Steel, 33 inches by 26.

SUBSCRIBERS to the above are respectfully informed, that Mr. HAWKINS will visit Halifax for the purpose of delivering their Copies; and to solicit the honour of the names of the Gentlemen of the City and Vicinity, who may be desirous of possessing a becoming memorial of the great conflict which planted the Royal Standard of the United Kingdom upon the Walls of Quebec, and dyed the plains of Abraham with the blood of WOLFE.

This Work has been honoured with the most distinguished approbation and patronage in Great Britain, and more than a thousand Subscribers in Quebec and Montreal; at the head of whom stand the names of

Her Most Gracious Majesty,
Her Majesty Queen Adelaide,
Field Marshall H. R. Highness Prince Albert,
Field Marshall, H. R. H. the Duke of Cambridge,
The Right Hon. the General Commanding-in-Chief.
His Excellency the Right Hon. Sir Charles Bagot, K.C.B.
Lieutenant General Sir R. D. Jackson, K.C.B.
Lieutenant General Sir James McDonell, K.C.B. and K.C.H.
Lieutenant General Clitherow,
Major, General Sir Richard Armstrong, C.B.
The Mayor and Corporation of Quebec,
The Mayor and Corporation of Montreal,
The Mayor and Corporation of Kingston,
The Mayor and Corporation of Toronto, &c. &c.

Proof Impressions......

Halifax, Oct. 13.

The Nova Scotian,
October 13, 1842.

Courtesy of the Dalhousie
University Library, Halifax, N.S.

Thomas Colton Creighton

Apart from the official logs kept on board sailing ships, many masters, mates and seamen kept their own private journals or diaries. Much more detailed than the official reports, they describe life on board ships and include accounts of accidents, fights, dismastings and shipwrecks.

On January 15, 1843, Thomas Colton Creighton joined the barque *Rose* and set out on a voyage to the Pacific in search of sperm whales. His diary[2] kept during the three-year voyage, gives a splendid description of life on board ship and a detailed account of whaling.

Born on July 18, 1825, Thomas was the son of George Brinley Creighton and Isabel Ann Grassie and a nephew of both James G. A. Creighton and Thomas Ritchie Grassie, the two partners in the firm of Creighton and Grassie.

Three short excerpts from his diary are quoted.

Sunday 28 [April], 1844

In the midst of the Lunar on tuesday a large Whale hove in sight from the mast head, and in five minutes three boats were down and pulling toward him. He soon went down and in ¾ of an hour came up within ¼ of a mile of the boats. The mate soon fastened, and the Whale by way of retaliating sunk and nocked the bottom of his boat in. The third Mate fastened next, and lost his line, but when the Whale came up about one mile to windward, he spouted thin blood and being near the 2nd Mate, he got fast. In the meantime the Old Man (who generally stays on board till the last) lowered and pulled first for the Mate to see if anyone was hurt, and found him standing on the stern sheets of his boat holding on to the waft pole, and his crew sitting each on his thwart with the water up to their necks, but fortunately none were hurt. The boat was entirely out of sight. We left him to be picked up by the ship keepers, and pulled to the Whale, which was now about three miles to windward, and soon fastened while the 2nd & 3rd Mates were working on him, he turned up about 5½ oclock, after 2 hours hard work, in which time he stove one boat, sounded out the line of another, ran five miles with a third, and made the fourth pull after him, and died amidst the shouts of the boats crews about 8 miles N N W of Matthews Island.

Wednesday 8th of Oct, 1845

. . . HOMEWARD BOUND. And may God of his infinite mercy grant us a speedy, and as pleasant a passage home, as our voyage has been throughout. We have taken about 1400 Bbls. Sperm and 900 of Whale Oil and about 5000 lbs. Whale Bone which is more than an average of all the ships. I feel truly thankful to the Almighty as well as for Blessing me with health & happiness during the voyage.

Sunday 26th Octr. 1845

A Memorable day and one of thankfulness to the Almighty for the wonderful preservation of our ship and cargo, if not of our lives. Last night 'twas our middle watch and my "turnout" helm on from 11 to 1 o'clock. We had a pleasant breeze at last and was steering "full & bye" heading SSE. The night was beautifully fine and clear starlight. As the ship steered very easy I began to think of my home and those I dearly love (to whom I was hastening at the rate of about four Knots an hour) and building high castles in the air as to what I would do when I returned to them, when all at once I heard a strange noise which at first I took for the wind blowing through the rigging when luckily the thought of surf struck me. It is impossible for me to describe my feelings at that moment. My Castles fell and my frame almost shook but instantly recovering myself I told the Officer of the Watch (Mr Pierce) who was singing and sitting on one of the spars on the weather side. He walked over to leeward directly, and as he went I felt convinced of our danger and put the wheel up a couple of spokes to gather good way on the ship to be prepared for the worst. He had hardly got as far as the lee main swifter when he sang out *hard down your helm let go the jib sheets* which was instantly done and the ship came flying to the wind and showed me Christmass Island with a heavy surf not more than two ship lengths off. One single minute longer would have made us a total wreck. . . .

Thomas Creighton returned to Halifax on the *Rose* on March 11, 1846. Three years later he married Annie Albro. Thomas became a master mariner and was captain of a number of vessels owned by Creighton and Grassie. In the 1860s he was master of the *Beauty*, a schooner of 124 tons, built at La Have in 1856 and owned by James G. A. Creighton. The vessel left Puerto Rico in early February, 1862, but never reached Halifax. She was believed to have been lost in the vicinity of Herring Cove about the twenty-fifth of February. There were no survivors. Thomas Creighton had on board his young son, Frank. Six months after the tragedy, a son was born to Mrs. Creighton and named Thomas Colton Creighton after his father.

Thomas Colton Creighton

Oil on canvas.
Unsigned and undated.

Courtesy of Dr. Helen Creighton.
Dartmouth, N.S.

JOHN ROBERTSON'S

Steam Mill & Deal Wharfs, St. John, N. B.

Engraving.
Drawn by G. Smith.

Courtesy of the New Brunswick
Museum, Saint John, N.B.

Born in 1798, John Robertson came to Saint John in 1817. Within a few years he was a major ship owner and timber merchant and soon became one of the leading financiers of the city. He was appointed to the Legislative Council of New Brunswick in 1837 and held office until Confederation in 1867, when he was appointed to the Senate. He died in England in 1876.

This fine engraving (c. 1840) shows clearly a variety of ships, barques and brigs of the period. While Robertson's timber wharf was a large operation, this scene on a smaller scale would have been very common throughout the Maritimes.

Halifax Harbour

Drawn by W.H. Bartlett.
Engraved by R. Wallis.
Published by Geo. Virtue, 1842.

Famous for its magnificent harbour, Halifax rapidly became the commercial centre of the Maritimes. This splendid view by W. H. Bartlett shows the harbour from the Dartmouth side. The small craft with square sails were owned by local residents and were used to convey themselves and their goods across the harbour.

The paddle wheel steamer on the left is either the *Sir Charles Ogle* or the *Boxer*. The *Sir Charles Ogle* was built at Dartmouth in 1829 by Alexander Lyle and was the first steamer built in Nova Scotia. The *Boxer*, also built by Lyle, was launched in 1838. Both were ferries operating between Halifax and Dartmouth. The *Sir Charles Ogle* remained in service until 1895.

The Golden Age 1846-1867

This period in the history of shipbuilding in the Maritimes is certainly one of the most exciting and yet at the same time one of the most frustrating to study. It is the most exciting because of the extent of the shipbuilding industry and the degree of prosperity throughout the Maritimes. Since all the shipping registers are extant, there is accurate information on nearly 10,000 vessels built during these years.

It is one of the most frustrating because most of the business records of the builders, owners and agents have been destroyed. While a few paintings, plans and half-models are available, their numbers are relatively small in proportion to the number of vessels built. Since the majority of vessels were going to England, a study of their careers necessitates a study of British shipping registers.

The term "The Golden Age" suggests for most people the age of the clipper and the age of speed. The so-called clipper ship was not, however, a sudden invention, but an evolution of ship design developed separately in Great Britain and in the United States. The basic principles of the hollow bow and a high length-to-breadth ratio for speed appear in manuscript form as early as 1670.[1] During the eighteenth century the emphasis had been mainly on carrying capacity. However, by the early nineteenth century the pattern had slowly begun to change, and by the second decade speed was becoming an important factor in ship design. The round bow of the eighteenth century was giving way to the hollow bow and the sleek lines of the clipper.

The entrance of the Americans into British trade in 1849, the opening of the China sea trade, the gold rushes and the increase in emigration to Australia, Canada and the United States all created a demand for fast vessels. The clipper ship was not, however, entirely the result of trade requirements. It was to a large extent "the result of publicity and the mania for speed."[2]

"The clipper ship was not the highest development of sailing ship design, because of the emphasis placed on speed at the expense of cargo capacity and low operating costs."[3] While the designs were very beautiful, many of the vessels were structurally weak and over-sparred and were extremely expensive to operate. They required very large crews to handle the sails and, because many vessels were driven hard by their masters, the hulls were strained and dismastings were common. Since very few plans of the Maritime-built vessels have survived, it is impossible to say how many were fine clipper models. Many, however, gained fame for their speed and quick passages.

An advance in the design of the sailing ship was seen in the medium clippers of the early 1860s. The fine bow of the clipper was retained but the vessels were more beamy and adjustments were made to the sail plan. A compromise between speed, stability, structural strength and cargo carrying capacity was achieved. The longitudinal strength of the hulls was increased by the method known as diagonal strapping. There were many improvements, especially in windlasses and capstans. Wire rigging was also introduced as well as improved pumps and small winches for braces and sheets. These all contributed to make the vessels safer and more economical.

One of the most important changes in rigging of the mid-nineteenth century occurred with the introduction of the double topsail. As the size of vessels had increased, so had the size of masts, yards, and sails. Large vessels might have as many as four or five reef bands on the topsails. Reefing and furling these enormous sails in heavy weather was very difficult and often very dangerous work. As early as 1835 a system of double topsail yards had been introduced on small vessels in the North Sea, and six years later the first system was introduced in American vessels by Robert Forbes. In this arrangement the topmast was set abaft the lower mast and both topsail yards were hoisted when the sails were set. A similar system was also introduced into the United States by Captain Frederick Howes in 1853. The topmast was set in the standard position, the lower topsail yard was secured permanently to the lower mast cap and only the upper yard was hoisted or lowered.[4]

Another modification to facilitate reefing was the roller reefing system introduced by Henry Cunningham in 1850.[5] By this method the yard rotated as it was lowered and the sail was wrapped around it. This method was fairly widely adopted. A few other patents were taken out by other people. However, it was the double topsail system that became the most popular and was introduced in nearly all large vessels by the early 1860s.

A major change in the system of registration of vessels occurred with the Merchant Shipping Act of 1854. Series of official numbers were allocated to each port of registry and an official number was assigned to each vessel on its first registration. The official number remained with the vessel as long as it was under British registra-tion, although the port of registry and the vessel's name might change several times. Allocated with the official number was the four letter signal code known as the International Code Signal. These signal letters are especially useful when they appear in a painting as they often make positive identification possible.

As before, the names of the owners and the number of shares they held were listed on the shipping registers. Now, however, the subsequent changes of ownership were entered in transaction books and unless the vessels were transferred to another port they were not normally re-registered. Provision for vessels to proceed to England on a Governor's Pass was again included. Apart from changes in ownership, the changes in the vessel's tonnage, rig, or name were entered as endorsements on the shipping register.

Registers of Certificates of Competency and Certificates of Service for masters and mates were also kept by the Registrar of Shipping in London. Notifications of change of master were forwarded to London and endorsements made in the registry book. These records give extensive information on the careers of many Maritime captains who held British certificates.

Certainly one of the most useful publications of the Registrar of Shipping is the Mercantile Navy List, printed annually after 1857. While there is less information about the vessels than is found in Lloyd's or any other commercial register, it is a complete list of all vessels still on the registry books for any year.

One of the most important sources of material on shipping is the large quantity of ships' papers kept by the Registrar General of Shipping and Seamen from the early nineteenth to the early twentieth centuries. While these records consist primarily of crew lists and agreements, many log books of the period before 1874 are also found in these papers. Although now fragmented, they can be found in the Public Record Office and the National Maritime Museum in London, England, in various archives in Great Britain and at Memorial University in St. John's, Newfoundland.

The William Carson

The first vessel believed to have been built in St. Martins, New Brunswick, was the *Rachel*, a schooner of 79 tons, launched in 1803 by Daniel Vaughan, registered at Saint John and owned by D. & F. Vaughan. In the following years, James Moran built the *Thistle*, a schooner of 59 tons and in 1807 the *Lord Nelson*, a brig of 129 tons. In 1815 Moran built the *Waterloo*, a ship of 392 tons, for John Ward & Sons of Saint John. This was the first ship built at St. Martins.

While James Moran remained the principal shipbuilder, other yards were being established, including those of David Vaughan, George Marr, Jacob Bradshaw, William Vail, William Brown and Samuel Carson. David Vaughan built his first vessel in 1820, the *Rainbow*, a schooner of 38 tons. His first large vessel was the *Saint Martins*, a ship of 572 tons, which was launched in 1838. The *William Carson*, a barque of 342 tons, was built by David Vaughan in 1846, registered at Saint John and owned by David, Simon, William and Benjamin Vaughan, all shipwrights of St. Martins. She remained on the Saint John register until transferred to Shields, England in 1853.

This painting shows the *William Carson* in a gale, close-hauled on the port tack. Sail has been reduced by furling the fore and main topgallant and royal sails and the mizzen topsail and by reefing the fore and main topsails and the spanker on the mizzen. The men on the foredeck are taking in the jibs. However, she is losing her fore topgallant and royal mast and the fore topsail and mainsail are being blown out of their ropes.

The William Carson

Barque   342 Tons
Built in 1846 at St. Martins, N.B.,
by David Vaughan.
106.3′ x 24.3′

Oil on canvas.
Unsigned and undated.
Courtesy of the New Brunswick
Museum, Saint John, N.B.

Joseph Cunard

This account of the launching of the *Ferozepore* appeared in *The Gleaner* of Chatham on September 12, 1846.

Launch: From the building yard of the Hon. Joseph Cunard, at Chatham, on the morning of Wednesday last, a very beautifully modelled, and substantially built ship, of the burden of 955 tons, new measurement, named the Ferozepore. She is, we believe, the largest vessel ever built in Chatham. She went off the stocks in fine style, amidst the cheers of a large number of the inhabitants, who had collected to witness the pleasing sight. There are three other vessels in this extensive yard in the course of erection, one of which will be ready for launching in the course of three weeks or a month.

The ship was, in fact, the largest constructed at Chatham at that time. Joseph Cunard's largest vessel, however, was the *Louisa*, a ship of 1033 tons built at Bathurst, New Brunswick, the year before.

Joseph Cunard, brother of Samuel Cunard of Halifax, had moved to Miramichi with his brother Henry around 1820 as agent for S. Cunard & Company. In 1828 Joseph began purchasing vessels and sending them to England to be sold. In 1839 he bought the shipyard of Joseph Russell at Chatham and, with William Rennie as master builder, began building on a very large scale. Joseph Russell, in the meantime, moved his shipyard to Beaubears Island.

Within the next ten years William Rennie built over fifty vessels for Joseph Cunard at Chatham, Carleton and Bathurst. Other vessels were built at Richibucto and a number in Prince Edward Island.

Financed by his brother, Samuel, and other merchants in Halifax, Joseph Cunard worked and lived on a grand scale. There were rumours of financial difficulties when Henry withdrew from the company in 1841. However, it was a severe blow to the community when in 1848, as a result of careless business practices and extravagant living, Joseph was forced into bankruptcy. After the failure, he went to Liverpool, England, into a commission merchant business and died there in 1865. By 1871 the Cunard Company in Halifax had paid off all the outstanding debts.

The *Ferozepore*, a ship of 955 tons, was actually built for Michael Samuel, a merchant at Miramichi. The vessel was registered at Miramichi on October 10, 1846, owned by Michael Samuel and sold five months later to merchants in Belfast, Ireland. In 1854, now owned by Tobin & Son, the vessel was registered at Liverpool, England and remained on the Liverpool register for another ten years.

This painting shows the *Ferozepore* entering harbour. A pilot jack (the union flag with a white border) has been hoisted at the fore truck. The royals and crossjack have been furled and the mainsail and mizzen topgallant are being taken in. The vessel wears the Red Ensign at the spanker gaff and the Tobin house flag at the main truck. There is a signal hoist at the mizzen.

The Ferozepore

Ship   955 Tons
Built in 1846 at Chatham, N.B.
by William Rennie.
143.8′ x 30.2′ x 22.7′

Oil on canvas.
Unsigned and undated.
Courtesy of the Mariners Museum,
Newport News. Barlow Collection.

The Boadicea

The years 1846 and 1847 saw yet another boom in shipbuilding in Saint John and even larger vessels were constructed. In the peak year, 1847, eighty new vessels, including thirty-two ships and fifteen barques, were registered in Saint John. The largest of these was the *Forest Monarch*, a ship of 1542 tons built by Owens and Duncan. She was the largest vessel constructed in the Maritimes up to that date. William and Richard Wright built the *David Cannon*, a ship of 1331 tons, in that same year.

The *Boadicea*, a ship of 909 tons, was built by James Malcolm in 1847 at St. Mary's Bay, Nova Scotia. She was one of a number of vessels built on the Bay of Fundy coast of Nova Scotia and registered at Saint John. The list of Nova Scotia builders who were building for Saint John owners included James Delap and Francis Bourneuf, who had started in the early 1820s, at Granville; Christopher Specht of St. Mary's Bay; Isaac W. Doane of Salmon River; David, William and Weston Hall and Abram Young, also of Granville.

The *Boadicea* was owned by J. & R. Reed who were operating their own vessels out of Saint John. The vessel remained on the Saint John register for sixteen years. On December 1, 1863, she was abandoned at sea while on a voyage from Cardiff to Portland, Maine.

This interesting painting shows the *Boadicea* entering harbour. The vessel has been brought into the wind and is lying to with her reefed topsails taken aback. The fore and main topgallants and all sails on the mizzen have been furled. The three jibs and the fore and mainsails are being taken in.

The Boadicea

Ship   909 Tons
Built in 1847 at Saint Mary's Bay, N.S.,
by James Malcolm.
151.8′ x 30.0′ x 22.0′

Oil on canvas.
Unsigned and undated.
Courtesy of the New Brunswick
Museum, Saint John, N.B.

The Dundonald

Ship   1372 Tons
Built in 1849 at Saint John, N.B.,
by William and Richard Wright.
176.0′ x 34.5′ x 20.7′

Oil on canvas.
Unsigned and undated.
Courtesy of the New Brunswick
Museum, Saint John, N.B.

William and Richard Wright

From 1839 to 1855, two of the most important shipbuilders in Saint John, New Brunswick, were William and Richard Wright and to these two brothers must go the credit for building some of the finest and largest sailing ships constructed in Canada. During their sixteen years as shipbuilders they launched thirty vessels, at the rate of nearly two per year.

Many of their vessels were built for Liverpool owners, particularly Ferni Brothers, Willis & Company and Pilkington & Wilson who operated the White Star Line. In some cases the Wrights were part-owners and, in other cases, operated the vessels themselves. By 1857 Richard had moved to Liverpool, England, to conduct the business there and was later joined by his brother William. However, they continued to have vessels built for them, not only in Saint John, but in other parts of the province.

The three ships listed below, at the time of their construction, were the largest vessels built in the Maritimes. The *White Star* and the *Morning Light* were the two largest vessels built in New Brunswick and the largest built in the Maritimes until the consruction of the *William D. Lawrence* at Maitland in 1874.

Beejapore   Ship   1676 Tons
Built in 1851   182.4' x 36.2' x 29.4'

The vessel was transferred to Liverpool, England, and owned by Willis & Company with the Wrights maintaining a half-interest in the ship for the first year. In October 1867 she was sold to foreign interests and almost immediately purchased by Ferni Brothers, renamed *Viceroy* and once more registered at Liverpool. The vessel was burnt at sea on November 29, 1868.

White Star   Ship   2339 Tons
Built in 1854   258.6' x 40.0' x 28.0'

This vessel was registered at Liverpool in January 1855, owned by Pilkington & Wilson who operated the White Star Line, and put into the Liverpool-Melbourne emigrant trade. In 1869 she was purchased by Ferni Brothers who operated her until she was wrecked on December 24, 1883.

Morning Light   Ship   2377 Tons
Built in 1855   265.3' x 44.1' x 21.1'

The vessel was owned by the Wrights and remained on the Saint John, New Brunswick, register until 1867 when she was transferred to Liverpool, England. The vessel was sold to a German company in 1881 and renamed *J. W. Wendt*. On February 21, 1889, the vessel left Bremen, Germany, bound for New York. A month later on March 22, she went ashore three miles north of Barnegat, New Jersey, and became a total loss.

The *Dundonald*, a ship of 1372 tons, was launched in April, 1849. She was the Wrights' largest vessel to date, being only slightly smaller than the *Forest Monarch*, a ship of 1542 tons built by John Owens and John Duncan two years before. The *Forest Monarch* held the record of being the largest vessel built in the Maritimes until the construction of the *Beejapore*. The *Dundonald* was registered at Saint John and owned and operated by the Wrights until 1854 when she was sold to Ferni Brothers and registered at Liverpool, England. The ship was burnt on November 2, 1858.

The painting shows the *Dundonald* entering harbour. The royals and cross-jack have been furled and the mainsail is being taken in. The vessel wears the house flag of W. and R. Wright at the fore truck, and the Red Ensign at the spanker gaff.

The Clipper Ship Marco Polo

As she appeared in the Mersey after completion of her unparalleled voyages from Liverpool
to Melbourne and back in 11 months and 21 days including detention in Australia.

Ship   1625 Tons
Built in 1851 at Saint John, N.B.,
by James Smith.
184.1′ x 36.3′ x 29.4′

Lithograph.
Printed by Thomas Dove,
North Egremont, England.
Courtesy of the New Brunswick
Museum, Saint John, N.B.

The Marco Polo

The *New Brunswick Courier*, Saturday, April 19, 1851:

A large and elegant vessel, called the MARCO POLO was launched on Thursday morning last from the building yard of Mr. James Smith at Courtney Bay. He is also the owner. She has three complete decks, measures 1625 tons and her length aloft is upwards of 184 feet. We presume, that although not quite the largest, this splendid ship is probably the longest that has been built in this province. She is named after the celebrated Venetian traveller who discovered the coast of Malabar.

We regret to learn that after this fine vessel had got clear of her ways in launching, she touched the bank of the creek, and the wind blowing fresh at the time, went over on her beam ends, in consequence of which some of the persons on board were hurt. One boy saved himself by jumping overboard and swimming ashore. The vessel, we understand, was not injured.

This newspaper item gives an interesting account of the launching of the *Marco Polo*, without doubt the most famous vessel built in Saint John. She was, in fact, slightly longer than the *Beejapore*, launched two months before, but her registered tonnage was slightly less.

The *Marco Polo* sailed from Saint John on May 31, 1851, for Liverpool, loaded with timber and scrap iron. After a voyage to Mobile for a cargo of cotton she returned to Liverpool and was purchased by James Baines for the Black Ball Line. The vessel was then refitted for the emigrant trade.

The *Marco Polo* left Liverpool on July 4, 1852, with 930 emigrants and a crew of 60 men. Her captain was James Nicol Forbes, the famous "Bully" Forbes who, before leaving, had boasted that he would have the *Marco Polo* back in the Mersey within six months. The vessel arrived inside Port Phillip Head at 11 A.M. on September 18, 1852, a record time of 68 days. She had beaten the steamer *Australia* by a week!

On the return trip, the vessel left Melbourne at 5 A.M. on October 11, 1852, made Cape Horn on November 3, arrived off Hollyhead at 3 A.M. on Christmas Day and anchored in the Mersey on Sunday, December 26. The return voyage had been made in 76 days and the round trip had taken five months and 21 days. On several consecutive days she had averaged over 360 miles a day and had logged 17 knots for several hours on end.

The shipping world was astonished. As she lay in the Salthouse Docks, a large banner hung between the fore and main mast. On it was written, in large black letters, THE FASTEST SHIP IN THE WORLD.

The *Marco Polo* continued to make good passages and remained in the Australian trade for more than 15 years. In the 1870s she was registered at South Shields, owned by Wilson and Blain and put into general cargo carrying. In 1880 the *Marco Polo* was sold to a Norwegian company and put into the timber trade. On July 22, 1883, the vessel, leaking badly, was run ashore on Cape Cavendish, Prince Edward Island.

The *Marco Polo* is shown in this engraving entering the Mersey. Only the foresail, fore topsail and jib are set. The mainsail has been clewed up and the main topsail is being taken in. All other sails have been furled. The house flag of the Black Ball Line is being worn at the main truck.

EMIGRATION VESSEL.—BETWEEN DECKS.

Wood engraving.
Illustrated London News, May 12, 1851.

Courtesy of the Public Archives
of Nova Scotia, Halifax, N.S.

Many thousands of immigrants had arrived in North America during the last half of the eighteenth century. However, after the Napoleonic Wars and the depression that followed, the number steadily increased.

Wealthy cabin-class passengers travelled in reasonable comfort and often had excellent food. The vast majority, however, travelled steerage class. While conditions varied from vessel to vessel and many shipowners did much to make the passengers comfortable, most suffered indescribable hardship. Accommodations below deck were always crowded; berths two and three tiers deep lined the between decks. In these berths families ate and slept. In many cases they were not allowed on deck during the entire voyage, which might last eight to ten weeks. The steerage passengers also faced the problem of cooking their own food and keeping clean. During stormy weather, ventilation was almost nonexistent and the smell and the state of filth can hardly be imagined. Sickness and disease were rampant and many died on the voyage. In the 1830s and 1840s severe cholera epidemics swept the immigrant ships, as well as dysentery, measles and small pox. From time to time government regulations were introduced to try to improve conditions on board and limit the number of persons travelling in each ship. Quarantine stations were set up at the major ports but most of these were inadequate and poorly managed. During the height of the epidemics the stations were packed and many people had to sleep outdoors. A large number arrived absolutely destitute, and the streets of many cities and towns were lined with women and children begging for food.

The photograph on the right is a copy of the regulations relating to passenger-carrying vessels as outlined in the "Passengers' Act, 1855." This abstract was to be kept posted during the voyage in at least two conspicuous places between the passenger decks.

Item No. 7 stated that no sailing vessel was to carry more persons than one statute adult to every two tons. Item No. 10 specified the minimum number of lifeboats required. For a small vessel of 300 tons, which might carry 150 persons, there were only three lifeboats. For a large vessel of 1400 tons, which might carry 700 persons, there were only six lifeboats. Shipwrecks, in fact, took a heavy toll of lives, and when a disaster occurred the chances of survival were slim.

ABSTRACT
OF SO MUCH OF THE
"PASSENGERS' ACT, 1855,"
(18th and 19th VICTORIA, cap. 119),
AS RELATES TO
PASSENGER SHIPS sailing from any BRITISH COLONY.
(Prepared by Her Majesty's Emigration Commissioners, in pursuance of the 61st Section of the Act.)

By Order of Her Majesty's Emigration Commissioners,

S. WALCOTT, Secretary.

Colonial Land and Emigration Office,
6, Park Street, Westminster,
September, 1855.

N.B.—This Abstract is to be kept posted up during the Voyage, in at least two conspicuous places between the Passenger-decks. Any Person displaying or defacing it will be liable to a PENALTY not exceeding FORTY SHILLINGS.—See 61st Section of the "Passengers' Act, 1855."

Courtesy of the Public Archives of Prince Edward Island, Charlottetown, P.E.I.

James Yeo

The early 1830s saw the rapid rise of James Yeo as a landowner, general merchant and shipowner. In 1836 he built his first vessel, the *Cordelia,* a brigantine of 112 tons, and within a few years he was building on a large scale. Yeo quickly developed an enormous shipbuilding and ship exporting business and became one of the great robber barons of Prince Edward Island. His largest vessel was the *James Yeo,* a ship of 1081 tons built at Bideford in 1856.

Yeo's son William moved to Appledore and acted as an agent for his father in Great Britain. Two other sons, John and James, were also shipbuilders and continued building after their father's death in 1868. In 1869 James Yeo Jr. launched the *Palmyra,* a ship of 932 tons, one of the largest in the Yeo fleet.

James Yeo, however, was not the only person in Prince Edward Island building vessels and exporting them to Great Britain. The 1840s and 1850s saw the establishment of James Duncan, Lemuel Cambridge Owen, James, George and Ralph Peak, James College Pope, William Welsh, John Lefurgey and many others. All became important shipbuilders and shipowners, selling their vessels through agents in Great Britain.

The *Alma,* a barque of 356 tons, was built in 1854 at Port Hill by George Ellis. The vessel was registered in Prince Edward Island, owned by James Yeo and commanded by his son-in-law, William Richards. In October 1856 Richards bought the vessel from Yeo and owned her for another fifteen years. She was lost in the ice in the St. Lawrence River in November 1871.

This weather view of the *Alma* shows the vessel entering Naples Harbour. The royals and two of the jibs have been furled and the topgallants, and mainsail are being clewed up. In addition to the square mainsail, the vessel carries a loose-footed gaff mainsail which has been taken in.

The Alma

Barque   356 Tons
Built in 1854 at Port Hill, P.E.I.,
by George Ellis.
118.2′ x 23.6′ x 16.0′

Gouache.
Unsigned and undated.
Courtesy of Mr. Basil Greenhill,
London, England, and Kenneth Richards,
Charlottetown, P.E.I.

The Oliver Lang

A very beautiful ship called the OLIVER LANG was launched on yesterday from the building yard of Messrs. Brown and Anderson in Portland. She was built from a draught furnished by Oliver Lang Esq., Master Builder in Her Majesty's Dock Yard, in order to meet the views of Her Majesty's Emigration Commissioners in London. She measures 1230 tons, N.M. and 1275 tons, O.M.

She is named after the above mentioned gentleman, and is allowed by competent judges to be a most superior vessel.

This notice of the launching of the clipper ship *Oliver Lang* appeared in the *New Brunswick Courier* on December 3, 1853. The vessel, built for Messrs. McCalmont Bros. & Company of Liverpool, England, was not registered at Saint John but proceeded on a Governor's Pass to Liverpool to be registered. She sailed under the Black Ball Line and was employed in the Liverpool–Melbourne run.

In the fall of 1856 James Baines opened up trade with Wellington, New Zealand, and the *Oliver Lang* was the first of a regular line of packets which operated between Wellington and Liverpool. In 1857 she was credited with making the run in 68 days, an extremely good passage for the period. In 1859 she was blown ashore while at anchor at Wellington and was later broken up.

The sail and spar plan of the *Oliver Lang* and the body, sheer and the half-breadth plan are shown in the following pages. The mock quarter galleries, a common feature in the design of merchant vessels of the late eighteenth and early nineteenth centuries, are unusual in vessels of this period.

Oliver Lang
DIMENSIONS OF SPARS
(in feet)

Spars	Fore	Main	Mizzen
Mast — deck to truck	134	140	110
Lower mast — deck to cap	63	68	58
Topmast	49	49	37
Topgallant & royal	47	47	34
Lower yard	76	76	34
Topmast yard	60	68	43
Topgallant yard	46	46	34
Royal yard	38	38	27
Spanker boom			52
Spanker gaff			37
Jib-boom	78		

The Oliver Lang

Ship   1236 Tons
Built in 1853 at Saint John, N.B.,
by Walter Brown.
182.7′ x 34.8′ x 23.0′

Original Plan: courtesy of the
New Brunswick Museum, Saint John, N.B.
Traced by Thomas Lackey and
Charles A. Armour, Halifax, N.S.

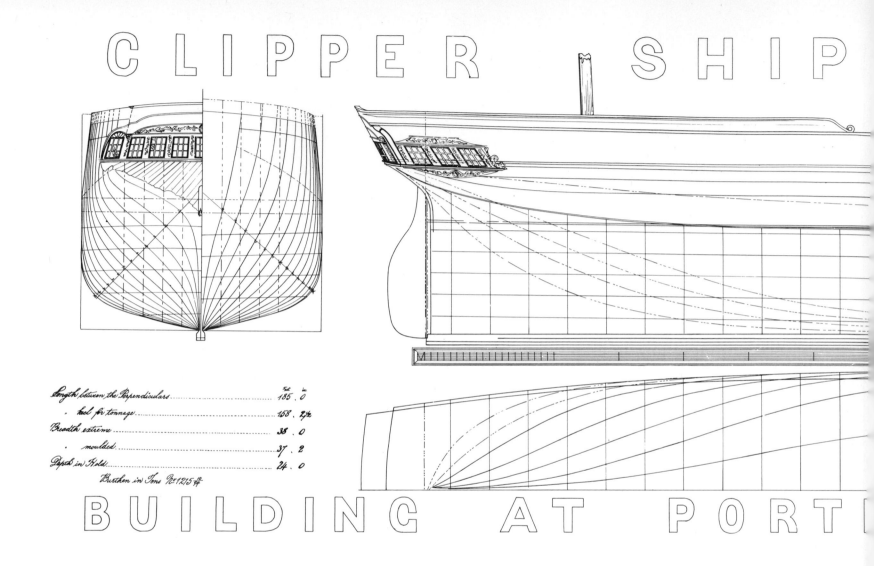

Length between the Perpendiculars .... 185 . 0
  . keel for tonnage .... 158 . 2½
Breadth extreme .... 38 . 0
  . moulded .... 37 . 2
Depth in Hold .... 24 . 0
    Burthen in Tons No 1215 42/94

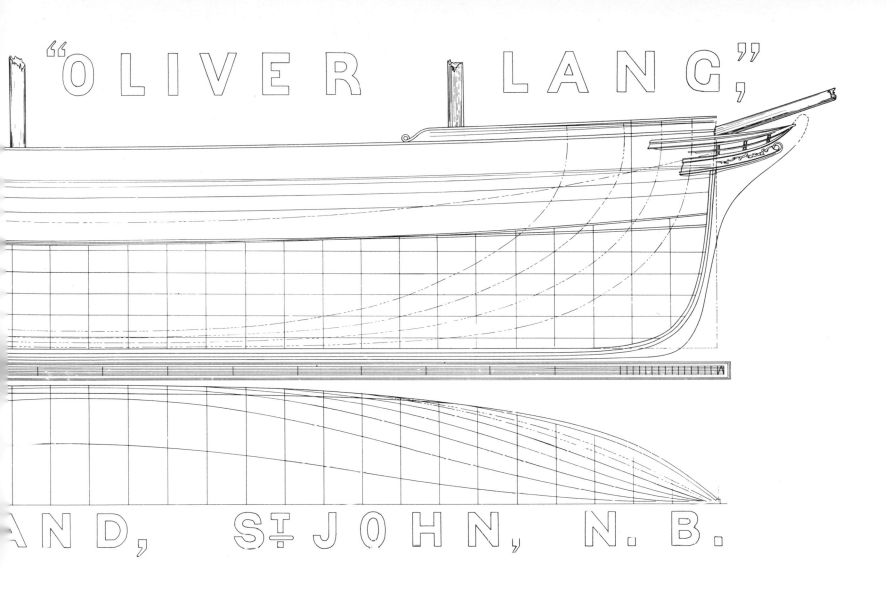

"OLIVER LANG,"

...AND, ST. JOHN, N.B.

Original Plan: courtesy of the
New Brunswick Museum, Saint John, N.B.
Traced by Thomas Lackey and
B. Renton Goodwyn.

The S. L. Tilley

A very superior new ship, called the S. L. TILLEY was launched from the building yard of Messrs Seely and Roberts, at the Straight Shore, where she was built under the superintendency of Mr. Thomas Morgan, who is well known as a faithful builder. This vessel has been built under special survey, and will class seven years at Lloyd's before leaving this port, and we understand, that for excellent workmanship, good materials, and a strong frame, she has not been surpassed by any vessel ever built in this Province. She was iron kneed on the stocks, the iron knees being of the strongest description and manufactured by Messrs Harris & Allen of this city. . . . She has been named after our deservedly popular ex-Provincial Secretary, and the vessel carries a full length figure head, which is generally thought to be a very good likeness of the gentleman after whom she has been named.

This description of the launching of the S. L. Tilley appeared in the New Brunswick Courier on July 6, 1856. The vessel was registered at Saint John and owned by George W. Roberts, Richard Seely and David V. Roberts.

A fascinating and often amusing account of life on board a sailing ship is given in the logbooks[6] of the S. L. Tilley from 1856 until 1858, parts of which are quoted here.

The ship sailed from Saint John on July 29, 1856, and arrived in Liverpool on September 18, a passage of more than seven weeks. By October 3 she was loaded and ready to return to Saint John.

> Oct. 3, 1965   Fresh Breeze & Squally
> At 6 AM halled to the dock gates at noon the piloott came on Board took steam and proceeded out of the harbour   At 3 PM got ashore on the sands tide falling tried for to get her off with two steamers but could not   Ship layeing Easey and taking no hurt   the Captain went to town in the steamer.
> Sat. 4   Fresh Breeze and Squally
> at 1 AM the steam tug came alongside with the captain and towed the ship off and went up in the river. . . .

When they arrived at Saint John on November 19, five of the crew deserted the ship and four men were discharged. The S. L. Tilley left Saint John on January 6, 1857, for Liverpool and soon ran into dirty weather.

> Jan 16   8 AM   Begins strong gales in the top galant sails   1 PM Sprung the Jiboom   Stowed the jibs & reefs in the topsails stowed the M.S.   4 PM increasing gales & rain 3 reefs in the topsails   Midnight   Continues strong gales & rain   heavy sea Ship Labouring heavy   6 AM Moderate & clear out all reefs & set top galant sails.

On March 19, 1857, while the S. L. Tilley was at Liverpool, the vessel was sold to Bowman Corning of Yarmouth who immediately took command. When the ship arrived at Halifax on May 2, 1857, ten of the crew deserted. On May 12, the S. L. Tilley was registered at Yarmouth and two days later Bowman Corning sold 43 shares to Thomas Killam. In November of the same year, the ship was loading at Montreal:

> Cargo took on board 300 deals, 600 Boards 76 Pairs of Oars, 8,278 Staves, 281 Barrels Fishes, 55 Barrels of Butter, 6,683 Barrels of Flour, 5,079 Bags of Wheat
> Loaded in Montreal to 17′ 6″
> Towed down to Quebec by Steamer J M′KENZIE with lighter SCOTLAND in tow with 2,238 Barrels of Flour loaded down to 19 ft. 2 in.   even keel

The vessel left Quebec on November 7 and arrived at Liverpool on December 7.

In September, 1858, the ship was back in Quebec, this time discharging iron:

> Sept 22   Throughout Fresh Westerly Winds and cloudy weather fore part crew employed variously   latter part discharged 220 Flat Bars and 446 Bundles Iron
> Noon the Cook went on shore without leave and shortly after returned drunk and obstructed the work of the Ship and I ordered him to keep quiet and go out of the way   he used most filthy language and finally struck and gave me a black eye   he afterwards went to sleep and remained quiet
> Sept 23   discharging 771 Bars and 200 Bundles Iron   Noon the cook drunk and the dinner spoilt and frequently going on shore and returning creating a great disturbance and rolling about the decks. In the evening he knocked the steward down & cut his head   sent for the police and had him locked up for the night
> Sept 25   Moderate SW Winds & clear throughout   Crew employed with the cargo and unbending sails.. Discharged 152

The S. L. Tilley

Ship   785 Tons
Built in 1856 at Saint John, N.B.,
by Thomas Morgan.
160.8′ x 33.6′ x 20.4½′

Watercolour.
Unsigned and undated.
Courtesy of the Public Archives
of Nova Scotia, Halifax, N.S.

Bundles iron & 175 railway bars   sent royal & topgallant yards down   unbent Fore and Mizzen topsails and courses. At 10 AM the cook was brought on board & returned to duty. In the evening he left the ship without leave.

Sept 26 [Sunday]   At 6 AM the Cook drunk in the galley and duty neglected   took three bottles of rum out of the galley and gave him in custody of the police   remainder of the day crew at rest . . .

Sept 27   The Cook was before the magistrate & sent to prison. . . .

The *S. L. Tilley* was owned by Thomas Killam and Bowman Corning until 1867. On July 29 she sailed from Savannah, Georgia, with a cargo of timber, bound for Liverpool, England. On August 2, during a hurricane, the ship was dismasted and became waterlogged. Seven members of the crew were washed overboard and lost. The rest of the crew were saved and taken to New York. The vessel and cargo were insured for $16,400.

The watercolour of the *S. L. Tilley* is especially interesting because it shows the vessel with double topsails on the main only. Since the illustration is not dated, it is impossible to say whether or not this was a feature of her original design.

The General Williams

Carved figures, ornaments and scrolls have decorated sailing ships for thousands of years. Many vessels, especially large ones, had finely carved figures. Others had a simple scroll or billet head. The importance of the figurehead for identification purposes, is indicated by the fact that there has always been a notation on the shipping registers as to the type of figurehead on the vessel. While a few of the figurehead carvers are known, the names of most of them have been lost. Very few of the figureheads themselves have survived.

The illustration shows the figurehead of the *General Williams*, a ship of 645 tons built at Grand River, Prince Edward Island, in 1856. It is a bust of Sir William Fenwick Williams, a native of Nova Scotia and a British General who, in 1856, returned to England from the Crimea as the "Hero of Kars." Among the many honours bestowed upon him was that of having three Maritime and five British vessels named after him.

The *General Williams* was registered, not in Prince Edward Island, but at Halifax, and was owned by a group of Halifax merchants. On the night of January 5, 1858, while on a voyage from St. Stephen, New Brunswick, to Liverpool, England, the vessel went ashore on the rocks near the mouth of Cutler Harbor, Maine, and was lost.

Figurehead of the ship General Williams

The Samuel P. Mussen

The *Samuel P. Mussen*, a brigantine of 212 tons, was built at Argyle, Nova Scotia, in 1856 and registered at Yarmouth on June 4 in the same year. Her original owners were:

Lemuel Robbins of Yarmouth	Master Mariner		16 shares
Prince Durkee	"	" "	32 "
Benjamin Ellenwood	"	" "	16 "
			64 shares

A list of her changes in ownership, noted on the shipping register,[7] is given below. It is a good example of the transaction system introduced in 1855.
Transactions:

Nov. 4, 1857   Benjamin Ellenwood sold 8 shares to George James Goudey of Yarmouth, Shipowner.

Aug. 6, 1857   Prince Durkee died; 32 shares went to Jane Durkee, Widow, and Dennis Crosby, Yeoman, both of Yarmouth.

Jan. 14, 1859   Jane Durkee and Dennis Crosby sold 16 shares to James Harvey Vickery of Yarmouth, Mariner.

Jan. 20, 1859   Jane Durkee and Dennis Crosby sold 8 shares to Robert Ellenwood of Yarmouth, Trader.

Jan. 25, 1859   Robert Ellenwood sold 8 shares to Dennis Crosby of Yarmouth, Carpenter.

By this time the owners of the vessel were:

Jane Durkee & Dennis Crosby	8 shares
George James Goudey	8 shares
Lemuel Robbins	16 shares
Benjamin Ellenwood	8 shares
James Harvey Vickery	16 shares
Dennis Crosby	8 shares
	64 shares

On July 25, 1861, a power of attorney was issued to James Harvey Vickery, Master Mariner . . . "to sell the Ship for a sum not less than twelve hundred pounds sterling at the port of Belfast or at any other Port or place in Her Majesty's Dominions within nine months from date of certificate."[8] However, the vessel was not sold. The closing entry on the register states that she was lost in June, 1862.

During the late eighteenth and early nineteenth centuries a new type of rig had developed. This was essentially the eighteenth century brigantine but without the square maintopsail and topgallant. The terms hermaphrodite brig, half brig and schooner brig occur frequently in the early nineteenth century shipping registers and all appear to be used interchangeably to describe the new rig. Gradually these terms disappear and the old term brigantine is used exclusively to describe the innovation.

This painting of the *Samuel P. Mussen* shows clearly the brigantine rig of the period. The vessel is shown here at anchor at Smyrna (Izmir), Turkey. Her master was Prince Durkee. All sails are furled and the fore topsail, topgallant and royal yards are shown in the lowered position.

"Saml. P. Mussen" P. Durkee, Commander of Yarmouth N. S. at Smyrna 1857.

The Samuel P. Mussen

Brigantine   212 Tons
Built in 1856 at Argyle, N.S.
100.6' x 23.6' x 12.2'

Gouache.
By Raffaeli Corsini, 1857.
Courtesy of Mr. Robert MacKenzie,
Halifax, N.S.

The Beau Monde

From 1840 until the late 1850s James Moran continued to be the leading shipbuilder in St. Martins. Gradually, his son James H. Moran took over the yard and in 1856 launched his first vessel, the *Ocean Wave*, a ship of 890 tons. His output of vessels steadily increased. By 1874 he had built eighteen ships, nearly all over 1000 tons, as well as a number of smaller vessels. James H. Moran owned the vessels in partnership with his brother Robert Greer Moran and Robert Galloway, who operated the Moran Galloway Fleet from Liverpool, England.

In 1873 the *Prince Umberto*, a ship of 1400 tons, was built for Moran at Saint John by Joseph K. Dunlop. The following year Moran moved to Saint John and five more ships, all over 1400 tons, were built by Dunlop for the Moran Galloway Fleet before Moran's death in 1877. Another vessel, the *King Cedric*, a ship of 1297 tons, was built for them by John Calhoun in 1875 at Hopewell, New Brunswick.

The *Beau Monde*, a ship of 1047 tons, was built by James H. Moran in 1857. The vessel remained in the Moran Galloway Fleet until 1881 when she was sold and registered at North Shields, England.

The following statement, taken from a Statement of General Average,[9] describes a voyage of the *Beau Monde* in 1865.

The vessel sailed from Bombay for Liverpool on the 8th of February, 1865 with a cargo of Cotton and Sundries. On the 23rd there were strong gales, with heavy thunder and lightning and at 6 a.m. the foretopmaststaysail was split. From this time up to noon of the 25th, they had strong gales, with hard squals, and a heavy cross sea running. At 10 p.m. the lower foretopsail was split, and at 10:30 p.m. the vessel broached to, with her head to the southeast, and at the same time the maintopsail was split. On the 26th the main trysail was blown away. It then blew a complete hurricane, and the vessel was thrown on her beam ends, with the lower yard arms in the water, and the maintopgallantmast was carried away, as well as the foreyard in the slings. Owing to the perilous position in which the vessel was placed, it became necessary to cut away the mizentopmast, when the foretopmast and the jibboom were carried away in the caps, the foretopmast backstays having been previously cut away. Every exertion was made to cut away the wreck from alongside, to prevent injury to the bottom, but without success. The starboard boat was also discovered to be gone. All hands were kept at the pumps, and the hurricane continued to rage with unabated fury to 5 p.m. when the weather moderated a little.

On the 27th the rudder head was discovered to have been carried away, and on sounding the pumps the crew found 5 feet 8 inches of water in the well. . . .

On the 28th the vessel made water at the rate of about 4 inches per hour. During several subsequent days the crew were employed about the jurymasts and rigging. . . .

On the 15th of April a pilot was taken on board and shortly afterwards the ship was taken in tow by the Government Steamtug and brought up the harbour of Port Louis.

This painting shows the *Beau Monde* under weigh. The crossjack has been furled and the mainsail is being clewed up. The vessel carries Cunningham's roller reefing gear on the topsails. The Moran house flag is being worn at the main truck. The five signal flags hoisted at the mizzen truck are not the vessel's official signal letters and are presumably a commercial signal code.

The Beau Monde

Ship   1047 Tons
Built in 1857 at St. Martins, N.B.,
by James H. Moran.
179.6′ x 36.4′ x 22.7′

Oil on canvas.
Unsigned and undated.
Courtesy of Byard A. Moran,
St. Martins, N.B.

The Mary E. Ladd

Brigantine   148 Tons
Built in 1861 at Meteghan, N.S.,
by Byron Ladd.
90.0′ x 24.0′ x 12.0′

Gouache.
Unsigned and undated.
Courtesy of the Yarmouth County
Historical Society and
Miss Kathryn Ladd, Yarmouth, N.S.

The Mary E. Ladd

The painting on the left shows the *Mary E. Ladd*, a brigantine of 148 tons, entering Naples Harbour. This view from the weather side shows clearly the rigging details of a brigantine during the last half of the nineteenth century. The vessel is square-rigged on the foremast and fore-and-aft-rigged on the main. She carries double topsails.

The *Mary E. Ladd* was built at Meteghan in 1867 by Byron Ladd, registered at Yarmouth and owned by Hubbard Davis of Westport, Nova Scotia. The vessel was lost off the Irish coast near Wexford on October 15, 1876.

The Frank

On the right is the Certificate of Registry of the *Frank*, a schooner of 92 tons, built at Mira Gut in the Island of Cape Breton by John Beaton in 1862, and registered at Sydney on August 23, 1862. It contains the vessel's specifications and a list of owners. In the top left-hand corner is the official number of the vessel which was carved into one of the beams and used for identification purposes as long as the vessel was under British registry.

This copy was carried on board the vessel and is especially interesting since it includes the name of the builder, which during this period was normally not included on the port copy of the register, or on the copy sent to London.

Courtesy of the Public
Archives of Nova Scotia,
Halifax, N.S.

Sackville, New Brunswick

A number of vessels were built in the Sackville area during the late eighteenth century. One of the first of these was the *Hope*, a schooner of 68 tons launched at Westmoreland in 1790, registered at Saint John on December 3, 1790, and owned by Samuel Gray and William Allan.

Shipbuilding steadily increased during the first quarter of the nineteenth century. The first of the major shipbuilders were four members of the Boultenhouse family: Bedford, Christopher, John and William. In 1824, Bedford Boultenhouse built the *Charlotte*, a brig of 128 tons, and the following year Christopher built the *Rebecca*, a schooner of 68 tons. Within the next few years the names of John and William also appear on the registers. Whether they built in the same yard is not known, but they appear to have operated their businesses separately.

Christopher, by far the most active, is believed to have started his shipbuilding in Wood Point and moved to Sackville around 1840. In 1841 he built his first large vessel, the *Lord Wellington*, a barque of 732 tons, and from then onwards his ouput steadily increased. He operated a number of the smaller vessels himself and a few of the larger ones were built for local ownership. Most, however, were constructed for English and Irish owners. In 1875, after fifty years as a builder, he launched his last vessel, the *Gem*, a brigantine of 281 tons.

George Anderson, a master mariner, also built a number of vessels at Sackville. The *Bella*, a schooner of 45 tons built in 1859, was probably his first. His last was the *Assyria*, a barque of 724 tons built in 1872 for Taylor Brothers of Saint John. On August 29, 1863, Anderson launched his new brig, the *Tantamar* of 386 tons. She was registered at Saint John on September 28 and owned by a group of traders of Saint John including George Anderson, who was also the master.

On March 31, 1867, the vessel was stranded on Cay Breton, off the coast of Cuba, and was a total loss.

The *Tantamar* represents a small brig of this period. Often locally owned and used extensively for the West Indies and coastal trade, as well as the European trade, this rig was very popular throughout the Maritimes. This painting shows the *Tantamar* under full sail entering Leghorn in August, 1864. The brig carries double topsails, topgallants and royals, two staysails (main topmast staysail and main topgallant staysail), and three jibs (inner, middle and outer). The deck detail is exceptionally fine.

Brig "Tantamar" of S. John N.B. Geo. Anderson Com.der Entering Leghorn August 1864.

The Tantamar

Brig   386 Tons
Built in 1863 at Sackville, N.B.,
by George Anderson.
117.0′ x 28.5′ x 17.2′

Watercolour.
By L. Renault, 1864.
Courtesy of the New Brunswick
Museum, Saint John, N.B.

The *Maggie Hammond*

The 1860s saw an increase both in the size and the number of vessels built in Yarmouth County as Yarmouth rapidly expanded as a shipbuilding community. Prominent shipowners included Thomas Killam, William D. Lovitt, Loran Baker, Amasa Durkee, Dennis Horton, A. C. Robbins, Thomas Allen, William Law, Hugh Cann, Freeman Dennis and George Doane.

In 1863, a peak year in shipbuilding, forty-two new vessels, including six ships and seventeen barques, were launched. Nearly all of the ships and barques were over 500 tons, the largest being the *Alexandra*, a ship of 889 tons built by Reuben and Benjamin Raymond for A. C. Robbins.

On September 3, 1863, the following notice appeared in the *Yarmouth Herald*:

> New vessel: The Barque MAGGIE HAMMOND, was launched from the shipyard of her owners at Meteghan on the 14th ult. She is 522 tons register and 640 O.M. and was built under the superintendance of Mr. Griffith Jenkins for Messrs. A. Durkee & Son. She is iron kneed and classed A1 at Lloyd's and is in all respects a superior vessel. She is to be commanded by Capt. Gideon Anderson, late of the barque GEORGE DURKEE.

The *Maggie Hammond* remained on the Yarmouth Register under the ownership of Amasa Durkee until 1875 when she was sold to foreign subjects.

A summary[10] of the vessel's voyages in 1869 and 1870, taken from the *Yarmouth Herald*, appears below:

Arrived New York 30-1-69 from Alicante. Capt. Willis
Cleared New York 12-2-69 for Galveston
Cleared Galveston 10-4-69 for Liverpool
Arrived Liverpool 25-5-69 from Galveston
Cleared Liverpool 19-6-69 for Philadelphia
Spoken 26-6-69 Lat 49°N Long 15°W from Liverpool for Philadelphia. Capt. Willis
Arrived Philadelphia 13-8-69 from Liverpool
Cleared Philadelphia 21-9-69 for Belfast
Arrived Belfast 4-11-69 from Philadelphia
Reported Bark Maggie Hammond at Belfast 4th November from Philadelphia — reports having been struck by a heavy sea on October 9th which stove in one of the boats.
Arrived Androssan 26-11-69 from Belfast. Capt. Scott
Arrived Lamlash 17-12-69 from Androssan. Capt. Scott
Cleared Lamlash 21-12-69 for New Orleans. Capt. Scott
Arrived New Orleans 10-2-70 from Androssan
Cleared New Orleans 30-3-70 for Liverpool
Arrived Liverpool 13-5-70 from New Orleans
Cleared Liverpool 26-6-70 for New Orleans. Capt. Flynn
Arrived South West Pass. 28-8-70 from Liverpool
Cleared New Orleans 4-10-70 for Liverpool
Sailed New Orleans 20-10-70 for Liverpool
Arrived Liverpool 13-12-70 from New Orleans

This watercolour by L. Renault shows the *Maggie Hammond* entering Leghorn in 1865 and signaling for a pilot. Sail is being reduced as she comes into the harbour. The mainsail has been clewed up and the outer jib and two of the staysails are being taken in. The fore topgallant and main royal yards are being lowered so that the sails can be clewed up. The vessel carries double topsails on the fore and main, and wears the Amasa Durkee house flag at the main truck. The signal hoist at the mizzen truck is not the vessel's official signal code.

Bark "Maggie Hammond", of Yarmouth N.S. G. Anderson Master. Leghorn 1865.

The Maggie Hammond

Barque   522 Tons
Built in 1863 at Meteghan, N.S.,
by Griffith Jenkins.
145.0′ x 31.0′ x 17.0′

Watercolour.
By L. Renault, 1865.
Courtesy of the Yarmouth County
Historical Society, Yarmouth, N.S.

The Maria Scammell

The *Maria Scammell*, a barque of 394 tons, was launched on June 4, 1864, at Carleton, New Brunswick. Two weeks later the *New Brunswick Courier* published this account of the event:

The "Marie Scammell" launched from the yard of Mr Joseph H Scammell, Sand Point is a very fine vessel built of large size timbers, selected with great care, perfectly free from sap and well seasoned. She is intended for the Valparaiso trade, is of good model and large capacity. She is yellow metal fastened and was fully iron kneed and ridered on the stocks: her dimensions are 124 feet in length, 28 ft 11 in breadth of beam and 16 ft. 9 in. depth of hold registering 394 tons. This vessel was built under Lloyd's special survey will be fully supplied with anchors, chains and general supplies and will have her classing certificate of 7A1 before sailing hence. She will be commanded by Captain Mussells. We wish her enterprising owners every success.

Joseph H. Scammell began as a shipbuilder in the early 1860s in partnership with Edward Darrel Jewett. Later he was joined by John Walter Scammell and Charles Edward Scammell and the company became known as Scammell Brothers. The *Maria Scammell*, one of their early vessels, remained in the Scammell fleet for twelve years. In 1876 she was condemned as unseaworthy and sold at public auction at Gibraltar.

This watercolour of the *Maria Scammell* was done by Edward Russell in 1869. The vessel carries double topsails. The fore and main royals have been furled and the fore topgallant is being taken in. The Scammell house flag is being worn at the fore truck.

The schooner on the right is the *Tropic Bird* of 139 tons, built at Carleton and launched on June 4, 1863. She was one of the first vessels owned by Joseph H. Scammell and was probably built by him. In December, 1872, the vessel was stranded at White Head, Rockland, Maine. She was later sold to American citizens and renamed *Nellie Cushing*.

Edward John Russell was born on the Isle of Wight in 1832 and came to Saint John, New Brunswick, in 1852. Later he moved to Fredericton and between 1857 and 1862 did a number of sketches for the *Illustrated London News*. After his marriage to Julia Marsh in 1862 the couple moved to Saint John. Russell did many sketches, marine paintings and cartoons and soon became involved in numerous projects. In 1872 he did illustrations for the *Canadian Illustrated News*.

After his wife's death in 1880 he went to Boston, travelled widely and remarried. He returned to Saint John and, from 1893 until 1895, did illustrations for the *Daily Telegraph* before returning to the United States. He died on September 1, 1906, at Dorchester, Massachusetts.

Russell is best known for his marine paintings which are especially valuable because of their fine technical detail. Because he often painted vessels from the builder's plans, they are extremely accurate. A view of Partridge Island, at the mouth of Saint John Harbour, was included in many of his ship paintings, and in others a small steamer was visible.

The Maria Scammell

Barque   394 Tons
Built in 1864 at Carleton, N.B.,
by Joseph H. Scammell.
124.0' x 28.9½' x 16.7'

Watercolour.
By Edward Russell, 1869.
Courtesy of the New Brunswick
Museum, Saint John, N.B.

HALIFAX AND BOSTON
SAILING PACKETS,
Old Established Line.

LAWSON, HARRINGTON & CO.,

AGENTS FOR THE

Halifax and Boston Packets,

GENERAL and COMMISSION MERCHANTS, and Dealers in

FISH, OILS, SALT, BREAD STUFFS, TOBACCO, TEA,

WEST INDIA PRODUCE, etc.,

COMMERCIAL WHARF,

HALIFAX, N. S.

Barque HALIFAX,......... Captain B. O'Brien,..........220 tons.
Brig AMERICA,............... " A. French, ...230 "
Brigantine BOSTON,......... " F. McGregor, ...120 "

These Vessels ply between Halifax and Boston, and Boston and Halifax, with the utmost regularity, one Vessel leaving each Port every week.

For Freight or Passage, having SUPERIOR ACCOMMODATIONS,

Apply to **LAWSON, HARRINGTON & Co.,**

HALIFAX, N. S.,

And CLARK & WOODWARD,

Fort Hill Wharf,
BOSTON.

THOMAS E. RYER.

The subscriber takes Contracts for

BUILDING VESSELS

Of all sizes, and guarantees that his workmanship will be equal to any in this Province.

Also, the Materials will be of good quality.

THOMAS E. RYER.

SHELBURNE, N. S.

ALLEN & CO.,

SAIL MAKERS,

LIVERPOOL, N. S.

DEALERS IN

CANVASS. ROPE, etc.   Also, all kinds of Galvanized Iron Work connected with the Trade.

A. V. ALLEN.   W. B. COBB.

These advertisements for Nova Scotia businesses appeared in the *Nova Scotia Directory*, 1864.

Courtesy of Mrs. Ian Manning.
Wolfville, N.S.

The Cherokee

The *Cherokee* represents one of the many vessels built in the United States and registered in the Maritimes after the repeal of the Navigation Act in 1849. A schooner of 83 tons, she was built at "Vinal Haven" in 1847, registered at Pictou in 1851 and shortly afterwards transferred to Halifax. In 1854 the vessel was registered at Liverpool and later that year rerigged as a brigantine. At the time of the disaster she was owned by William Innes of Liverpool.

The brigantine *Cherokee* left Boston on Monday, January 16, with a full cargo, six crew and six passengers. The captain was Ambrose Dunlap. The *Liverpool Transcript* of January 26, 1865 gave this account of the wreck:

> On Wednesday night, during a thick snow storm and heavy sea, struck on a ledge off one of the Tusket Islands, vessel bilged, masts went by the board and rendering them completely helpless. From this perilous situation the vessel came off at flood tide and full of water

The wreck drifted all next day until 8 P.M. when she grounded on a ledge off Woods Harbour and began to break up. The passengers and crew remained on part of the wreckage all Thursday night and on Friday morning drifted out to sea. By this time they had been sighted by people on shore and two boats were launched. After several attempts, they were taken off and landed at Clark's Harbour, Cape Sable Island. Four of the passengers, Mr. and Mrs. John Guether, their three-year-old child and Mrs. Guether's mother, died from exposure.

The poem by Moses Nickerson was printed in the *Liverpool Transcript* on March 2, 1865.

Provincial Poetry.

For the Transcript.

Loss of the Cherokee.

BY MOSES NICKERSON.

The night was gloomy—lowering dark,
  Keen blew the howling blast,
While onward steer'd the fated bark
  On to destruction—fast,
Yet safe she bore her living freight,
  Whose hearts with hope beat high,
Unconscious of their coming fate
  Nor thought of danger nigh.

But hark ! there comes a dreadful crash,
  She strikes the hidden rock,
The waves in fury o'er her dash—
  She trembles 'neath the shock ;
The startled band, with fears impressed
  Rush wildly to the deck,
While consternation fills each breast,
  They view the helpless wreck.

All means of safety are denied,
  The deck apart is torn
And with it, on the heaving tide
  The sufferers are borne
Alone, far out upon the deep,
  Each refuge wrapt in gloom
And but a slender hold to keep
  Them from a watery tomb.

With mornings earliest misty gleam
  Their anxious gaze was bent
Upon the shore, far distant seen,
  But still no aid was sent.
Still with a lingering hope they prayed
  That heaven would them protect,
And in kind mercy to their aid
  Some friendly power direct.

But useless all, they watched in vain
  Until that day's sad close ;
And night more gloomy came again —
  A night of untold woes.
Still clung they to that wave-washed piece
  Wild on the billows tossed,
Unsheltered from the icy breeze—
  Their limbs benumbed with frost.

O what a dismal night was there !
  The agonizing wail—
The suff'rer's groans, the strong man's prayers,
  Rose mingling with the gale.
The tender mother in her arms
  Her infant did enfold
Fond to her pressed its lifeless breast,
  Her own fast growing cold.

The night—the long dark night at last
  Passed fearfully away,
And round o'er the dreary waste
  Slow spread the light of day.
Now He who reigns supreme on high
  And does the storm command,
Has heard the supplicating cry
  And succour is at hand.

To men on shore, far off appears
  An object dim and dark,
And anxious eyes, and hopes and fears,
  Its slow, strange progress mark.
As eagerly they now survey,
  The signal of distress
As waving o'er it seen, and they
  Too well its import guess.

Quick ! man the boats ! no time delay
  To rescue and to save,
The boats they urge swift through the surge
  With valiant hearts and brave.
The sufferers saw the boats draw near
  And with new hopes they gazed,
And then, with many a thankful tear,
  They murmured : God be praised.

Rescued !—then back again they haste
  With speed to reach the shore,
Alas ! of no avail to some
  Their sufferings are o'er.
The husband and the loving wife—
  The aged mother dear—
By death released, now rest in peace,
  Unknown to grief or care.

Cape Sable Island, Feb. 14, 1865.

Courtesy of Mrs. Hector MacLeod,
Liverpool, N.S.

The Bigelow Family

Various members of the Bigelow family built vessels in the Cornwallis township and vicinity for a period of more than one hundred years. In 1815, Ebenezer Bigelow Sr. built a small topsail schooner and continued building at irregular intervals until 1830.

Ebenezer Bigelow Jr. helped in several shipyards before joining partnership with Edward G. Lockhart and Joseph Northrup to build the *Sam Slick*, a brig of 143 tons, at Canning in 1840. The partnership, however, soon dissolved and Ebenezer continued on his own. Some of his vessels were designed by his brother Gideon. The two brothers in turn designed vessels for other builders. A number of their vessels were built at Parrsboro.

Ebenezer built for a number of merchants. By the mid-1850s he was taking shares in his vessels and eventually he operated many of them himself. By 1868 his son John E. had joined the firm which became E. Bigelow and Sons, and John E. is listed as the master builder after 1883. Their largest vessel was the *Calcutta*, a barque of 1282 tons built at Parrsboro in 1876. While they built several large barques and ships, the vast majority of their vessels were small schooners, brigs and brigantines of 100 to 200 tons.

In spite of the failure of the company in 1885, a number of two- and three-masted schooners were built by John E. The last vessel built in the Bigelow yard was the *Cape Blomidon*, a three-masted schooner of 408 tons launched by John E. Bigelow in 1919.

The *Fred Clark*, a brigantine of 146 tons, was built by Ebenezer Bigelow at Canning in 1865 and launched on October 5. The vessel was registered at Windsor, Nova Scotia, and owned by John H. Clark, George E. Eaton and the builder. She was lost on the coast of South America in 1868.

This tracing of the original spar plan of the *Fred Clark* shows clearly the rig of the brigantine or half-brig as it was sometimes called. The position of the mast and yards, the standing rigging and the deck houses are clearly shown. The foremast still carries a single topsail. The note in the upper left-hand corner, written by the builder, says: "This vessel was considered by the master after proving her to be perfect both in hull and sparring."

Fred Clark
DIMENSIONS OF SPARS
(in feet)

Spars	Fore	Main
Mast — deck to truck	90	94
Lower mast — deck to cap	40	58
Topmast	32′ 2″	45′ 9″
Topgallant and royal	35′ 3″	
Lower yard	55	
Topmast yard	42	
Topgallant yard	31	
Royal yard	23	48′ 4″
Spanker boom		30′ 6″
Spanker gaff		
Jib-boom	78	

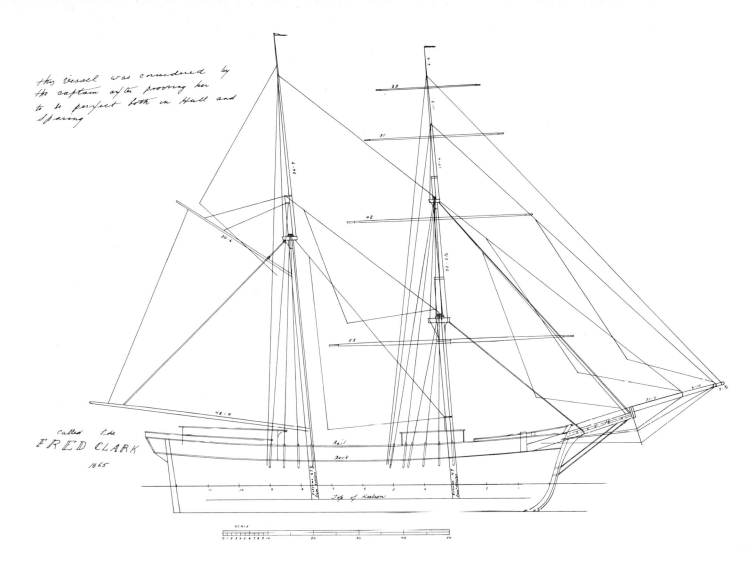

This vessel was considered by the captain after proving her to be perfect both in Hull and Sparring

called the
FRED CLARK
1865

The Fred Clark

Brigantine   146 Tons
Built in 1865 at Canning, N.S.,
by Ebenezer Bigelow.
87.0' x 24.0' x 10.2'

Original spar plan: courtesy of
Mr. John Bigelow, Halifax, N.S.
Traced by Charles A. Armour.

The Voyage of the Research

Thomas Killam began as a ship owner in 1830 with the purchase of the *Trinidad*, a brig of 160 tons built in 1830 by James Jenkins at Yarmouth. Gradually he increased the number of his vessels and by the 1850s had become one of the most prominent merchants in Yarmouth. One of his most famous vessels was the *Research*, a ship of 1459 tons built by J. Richards in 1861. She was the largest vessel to be built in Yarmouth up to that time and is reported to have cost her owner $65,000.

Some ships obtain fame through their fine lines, excellent sailing qualities or speed. Others, like the *Research*, gain fame through their disasters. In the winter of 1866/67, while on a voyage from Quebec to Greenock loaded with timber, the vessel was involved in one of the most grueling episodes in the history of Nova Scotia shipping, and Captain George Washington Churchill (later known as "Rudder" Churchill) became a famous man as a result.

This account of the incident is taken from the official report[11] made by Captain George Churchill when he arrived at Greenock.

> Sailed 10th November 1866 prosecuted the voyage without particular occurence until the 27th on which day at 8 p.m. strong gales reduced sail at a.m. gale increasing and very heavy sea running at 6 carried away jibboom guys bands and weather releiving tackls. At 7:30 a tremendous gale blowing with a very heavy sea the fore topmast staysail was blown away as were also the fore and main lower topsails the rudder stock broke off a little below the case and port rudder chains parted tried all possible ways to secure rudder and afterwards got a hawser round it taking in quarter pipes and hove well taut but this did not keep rudder still and it commenced to break in pieces as there was no possible means of securing rudder was obliged to throw overboard a portion of the cargo in order to lighten her aft so as to get tackles on it. 28th strong gales crew employed heaving cargo overboard until 6 P.M. set fore and main topmast staysails to give ship headway so as to prevent rudder from surging so heavily in stern port at 8 got a tackle on jib guys and set jib at midnight more moderate the hawser chafed off rudder which was still breaking in pieces. 29th got out rudder stock and a 4 A.M. the rudder was unshipped and towed alongside until 10 when it was got on board and had the iron taken off crew employed in making a rudder out of a spare spar and deals. At noon got old rudder put over again. Ship making a great deal of water from bow ports. 30th a very heavy gale, the main and main topmast stays were carried away. 1st December new rudder completed but was unable to ship it on account of the heavy seas, shipped a heavy sea which stove in wheel house. 2nd at 1 p.m. put rudder over side and got it shipped but at 7 p.m. the hawser which was securing it parted and the rudder was lost. . . .

For nearly two more months the crew shipped and unshipped jury rudders some eighteen times and lost three of them. A portion of the cargo of deal was thrown overboard to lighten the ship. Winds of hurricane force blew most of the time and stove in the forward house and locker, bulwarks, wheelhouse and main hatches. One of the pumps became choked with sand and a number of sails were blown away.

On the 28th of January, 1867:

> . . . crew employed in making a new rudder out of the other end of the main yard from this to 1st February experienced strong gales the new rudder being proceeded with. On later date more moderate. At 9 a.m. got rudder shipped and made sail. The footrope of main uppertopsail parted and split sail, crew constantly at pumps as the water was gaining on them. 3rd blowing a very heavy gale accompanied with a fearfully big sea causing vessel to labour heavily. 4th at 4 p.m. off Ailsa Craig and being apprehensive that the temporary rudder might have received damage during gale of previous day and might at any moment get adrift deemed it prudent for the general safety to engage the Tug Steamer COMMODORE to tow vessel to Greenock, accordingly the steamer took vessel in tow and on following day came to anchor at the Tail of the Bank notwithstanding that the pumps were kept constantly going it was found that the water in hold had increased to 9 feet and a gang of labourers were employed to pump ship out. The vessel was afterwards towed into the harbour at Greenock by two tug steamers and moored.

On the death of Thomas Killam in December, 1868, the ownership of the *Research* was transferred to Killam's four sons who continued to operate the Killam fleet. In October 1872 the vessel was sold to Le Baron Vaughan of Saint John and within a year passed to foreign ownership.

Born in 1850, Aaron Flint Churchill was a nephew of Captain George Washington Churchill and was the mate on board the *Research* in 1866. In 1872 he was mate on board the *B. Rogers*, a barque of 576 tons built at Tusket, Nova Scotia, in 1864 and registered at Yarmouth. At the age of twenty-seven he left the sea and established himself as a stevedore at Savannah, Georgia, dealing mainly in the cotton trade. Later he established the Churchill Line which he operated until his death at Savannah in 1920.

Aaron Flint Churchill

Courtesy of the Yarmouth
County Historical Society,
Yarmouth, N.S.

The Alice Roy

One of the first vessels built in the Maitland area was the *Trial*, a schooner of 72 tons, launched in 1810. Shipbuilding steadily increased although it was confined to small schooners and brigs. Shipbuilders in the 1830s and 1840s included Jacob Frieze, David Smith and Archibald MacCallum. One of the early merchants was David Frieze, who established a general store at Maitland in 1839 and was soon shipping timber to the United States. In the late 1860s he was joined by Alexander Roy and they established the firm of Frieze and Roy, still in operation today.

The first large vessel constructed at Maitland was the *Clyde*, a ship of 903 tons, built by William D. Lawrence in 1863; his ship *Pegasus*, built in 1867, was the first vessel over 1000 tons. Other major shipbuilders of Maitland from the 1870s to the 1890s include Alfred Putnam, A. A. MacDougall, Charles Cox, Archibald MacCallum, Joseph Montieth and Alexander Roy.

Two of the vessels built by Alexander Roy for Frieze and Roy were the *Snow Queen*, a barque of 994 tons built in 1872, and the *Trust*, a brigantine of 522 tons built in 1876. Both of these were operated by the company until 1889. Roy's largest vessel was the *Esther Roy*, a ship of 1533 tons built in 1877.

On October 1, 1866, Alexander Roy launched the *Alice Roy*, a barque of 610 tons. She was one of a number of his vessels in which William J. Stairs of Halifax was part owner. The managing owner of the *Alice Roy* was William Douglas, a master mariner of Maitland. On June 21, 1881, the vessel was wrecked on the Pilgrims in the St. Lawrence River, but was later repaired and registered at Quebec. She was abandoned in the North Atlantic in 1887.

The spar plan of the *Alice Roy* represents one of the many hundreds of medium-size barques built in the Maritimes during the 1860s. The fore and main yards, and the fore and main lower topsail yards are secured to the masts and do not move up and down. The fore and main upper topsail, topgallant and royal yards are shown in the lowered position which they take when the sails are furled. They are raised when the sails are set. The positions of the three jibs, five staysails, spanker and mizzen topsail are also indicated. Of particular interest is the arrangement of the studding sails, shown in the upper right-hand corner of the plan. They are drawn to half-scale.

Alice Roy
DIMENSIONS OF SPARS
(in feet)

Spar	Fore	Main	Mizzen
Mast — deck to truck	105	108	86
Lower mast — deck to cap	43	46	44
Topmast	39	39	49
Topgallant and royal	38	38	
Lower yard	61'6"	61'6"	
Lower topmast yard	55	55	
Upper topmast yard	52	52	
Topgallant yard	42	42	
Royal yard	33½	33½	
Spanker boom			37
Spanker gaff			27
Jib-boom	44		

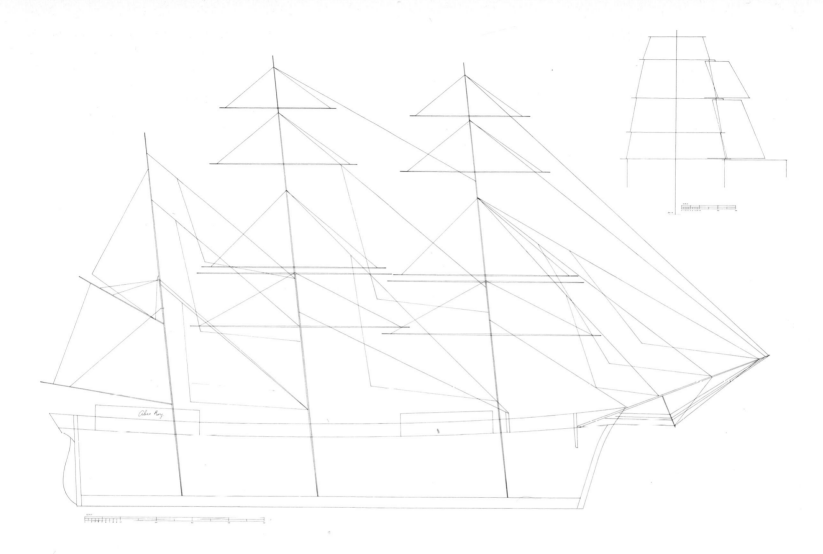

The Alice Roy

Barque   610 Tons
Built in 1866 at Maitland, N.S.,
by Alexander Roy.
152.6′ x 32.2′ x 18.8′

Original Spar Plan:
Courtesy of the Dalhousie
University Archives, Halifax, N.S.
Traced by Charles A. Armour.

The M. Wood

Mariner Wood, a prominent Sackville merchant, had vessels constructed for him by a number of builders, including Charles Dixon, Henry Purdy, and Edward Wood Ogden. His first vessel, the *Triumph*, a brigantine of 144 tons, was built by Charles Dixon in 1850 and in the following year Dixon built the *Sarah Louisa*, a small barque of 377 tons. From 1853 to 1856 Dixon built four large ships for Wood, all of which were sold in England. The largest of these was the *Sarah Dixon*, a ship of 1498 tons launched in 1856.

Henry Purdy's shipyard was located directly behind his house at Westcock. His first vessel was the *Merlin*, a small schooner of 79 tons, which he built in 1852 in partnership with Martin Cole. The Purdy yard continued in operation until 1878. On May 16, 1866, Henry Purdy launched the *M. Wood*, a barque of 550 tons named after its owner, Mariner Wood. The barque was owned and operated by Mariner and his son Josiah until sold at Charleston, South Carolina, in 1875.

From 1867 onwards, most of the vessels of the Wood fleet were built by Edward Wood Ogden at Port Elgin and Sackville. When Mariner Wood died in 1875 the business was continued by his son Josiah who had joined his father several years earlier. Five more vessels were built by Ogden for the Wood fleet. The largest of these was the *Kwasind*, a barque of 984 tons built at Sackville in 1878. Two years later, in 1880, Edward Ogden built the *Siddartha*, a barque of 463 tons, the last square-rigged vessel to be launched in Sackville. The *Siddartha* was owned by Josiah Wood for nineteen years until she foundered at sea on February 2, 1899.

Josiah Wood represented Westmoreland in the House of Commons from 1882 until 1895 when he was appointed to the Senate. From 1912 until 1917 he served as Lieutenant Governor of New Brunswick and died at Sackville on May 13, 1927.

This watercolour of the *M. Wood* gives a great deal of fine deck and rigging detail. The reef points on the spanker, used when reefing the sail, are clearly shown. The vessel carries double topsails, three jibs and six staysails.

The M. Wood

Barque   550 Tons
Built in 1866 at Sackville, N.B.,
by Henry Purdy.
139.0′ x 31.4′ x 17.6½′

Watercolour.
Unsigned and undated.
Courtesy of the New Brunswick
Museum, Saint John, N.B.

The John Mann

Bennett Smith of Windsor, one of the most prominent shipbuilders and owners of Hants County in Nova Scotia, began his shipbuilding career in 1839 with the construction of the *Matchless*, a brig of 168 tons. Another brig, the *Eclipse*, of 195 tons, was built the following year. After 1846 his output steadily increased and he averaged one vessel per year. His largest was the *Nile*, a ship of 1336 tons built in 1864. After 1869 a number of vessels were built for him in Saint John by John Stewart.

After 1877 Bennett Smith stopped building in Windsor and had vessels built for him by W. & R. Wallace at Gardner's Creek, Gaius Turner at Harvey, John Fraser at Saint John, New Brunswick, and Shubael Dimock at Windsor. After Smith's death in 1886 at the age of 77, the business was taken over by his sons, and another vessel, the *Loodiana*, a ship of 1820 tons and the largest of the Smith fleet, was built by J. B. North at Hantsport in 1889.

The *John Mann*, a ship of 1043 tons, was launched by Bennett Smith on June 1, 1867, and registered at Windsor on June 7. Bennett Smith, who was also the managing owner, held sixteen shares and the remaining forty-eight shares were held by ten other people from Windsor and Newport. On June 11, 1867, Bennett Smith sold four shares to Thomas Aylward for $2,385.50. This amount put a value of $38,168.00 on the vessel.

An indication of the profits made by the shareholders is given in the accounts of Thomas Aylward,[12] Master Mariner of Newport. A summary of the income Aylward received from his shares over the next seventeen years is shown in the following table.

As can be seen from the table, the vessel paid for herself after six years. On an initial investment of $38,000 the vessel made a profit of $78,500 over a seventeen-year period.

This painting shows the *John Mann* with all sails set except the crossjack, which has been taken in. The ship's signal letters, H.Q.T.K., have been hoisted at the monkey gaff.

ACCOUNTS OF THOMAS AYLWARD
Four Shares of the Ship *John Mann* purchased from Bennett Smith

1867		4 Shares	Total cost of the ship (64 shares)
	Cost in £	£596–5–11½	£9,536–15–4
	Cost in $	$2,385.50	$38,168.00

Income			
	Cash received	Total on 4 shares	Total for the Ship (64 shares)
1868	£102–4–2	£102–4–2	£1,635–6–8
1869	70–10–0	172–14–2	2,763–6–8
1871	39–1–3	211–15–5	3,388–7–8
1872	161–8–0	373–3–5	5,970–14–8
	£1 = $4.00	$1,492.68	$23,882.88
1873	$934.16	2,426.84	38,829.44
1874	446.10	2,872.94	45,967.04
1875	513.32	3,386.26	54,180.16
1876	278.91	3,665.17	58,642.72
1877	516.32	4,181.49	66,903.84
1878	639.51	4,821.00	77,136.00
1879	455.33	5,276.33	84,421.28
1880	513.59	5,789.92	92,638.72
1881	452.85	6,242.77	99,884.32
1882	57.21	6,299.98	100,799.68
1883	404.80	6,704.79	107,276.64
1884	219.42	6,924.21	110,787.36

Sale of vessel at New York November 1, 1884, for $7,000.00			
Share	367.62	7,291.83	116,669.28
Profit		4,906.33	78,501.28

The John Mann

Ship   1043 Tons
Built in 1867 at Windsor, N.S.,
by Bennett Smith.
178.5′ x 38.0′ x 24.0′

Oil on canvas.
By John Loos, undated.
Courtesy of Mr. John Kendell,
Windsor, N.S.

The Kelso

Prince Edward Island had seen a dramatic increase in ship-building after the late 1830s and vessels and timber were certainly its greatest exports during the middle of the nineteenth century. The greatest peak occurred in 1865. Of the 146 vessels registered that year on the Island, 126 were new vessels and approximately 70 per cent of these were transferred to England within a year. The largest vessel constructed in 1865 was the *Ocean Pearl*, a ship of 965 tons built by James Yeo at Port Hill and sold in Bristol the following year.

The preparation of the timber, both for building the vessels and for supplying their cargoes, as well as the construction of the vessels themselves utilized most of the labour force available. As long as good wages could be obtained in the lumber camps and shipyards, the clearing and cultivating of farm land was badly neglected. The failure to develop other industries certainly hindered the Island's adjustment to a changed economic scene when the demand for wooden vessels began to fall off in the late 1870s.

Needless to say, the Island was also affected by the slump of the late 1860s and the production of vessels dropped considerably. One of the vessels built during this period was the *Kelso*, a topsail schooner of 80 tons built by John Douse at Souris in 1867. The vessel was registered at Charlottetown and was owned by the builder. In the following year she was sold to William Besley of Watchet and registered at Bridgewater, England. She was lost with all hands on January 26, 1883, near Falmouth, England.

In this watercolour by John Chidgey, the *Kelso* is shown under full sail close-hauled on the starboard tack.

Most marine artists specialized in painting square-rigged vessels under sail, and paintings of small coastal craft such as the *Kelso* are fairly scarce. A master mariner as well as an artist, Thomas Chidgey of Watchet, was one of the few to paint the small vessels trading around the south coast of England during the latter part of the nineteenth century. Many examples of his work have survived and provide a unique record of these vessels, a large number of which were built in the Maritime Provinces.

The Kelso

Topsail Schooner   80 Tons

Built in 1867 at Souris, P.E.I.,
by John Douse.

72.5′ x 22.0′ x 8.35′

Watercolour.
By John Chidgey, undated.
Courtesy of Mr. Basil Greenhill
and the National Maritime Museum, London.

Decline 1868-1900

From the point of view of the history of the Maritime Provinces, this period is perhaps the most interesting. Despite the great slump in 1867/68 and the general world depression that followed, the situation soon improved. Even though many British merchants were now turning to steam, and the demand for Canadian-built vessels was much less than before, the early 1870s saw the involvement of more and more Maritimers in the ownership of vessels. The result was a subsequent increase in shipbuilding. The last great peak in shipbuilding, which occurred in 1874, is summarized in the following table.[1]

Number of Vessels and Number of Tons Built
in Canada, 1874

	Vessels	Tons
New Brunswick	104	49,468
Nova Scotia	175	84,480
Prince Edward Island	89	24,939
Total for the Maritimes	368	158,887
Total for Canada	496	190,756

The peak year of Canadian ownership of vessels occurred in 1878. In that year Canada stood fifth on the list of shipowning countries of the world.

Number of Vessels and Number of Tons on
the Registry Books of Canada, 1878[2]

	Vessels	Tons
New Brunswick	1,142	335,965
Nova Scotia	3,003	553,368
Prince Edward Island	322	54,250
Total for the Maritimes	4,467	943,583
Total for Canada	7,469	1,333,015

A large number of paintings and photographs of this period have survived as well as half-models and a few spar plans. While much has been destroyed, considerable manuscript material is available in archives and in private hands in the form of family papers and business records. Much more material still lies hidden in attics and basements of old buildings awaiting either salvage or destruction. The importance of this material for the Maritime historian can not be overestimated. Since many people were becoming involved in vessel ownership, diaries and accounts are often the only indication of a vessel's cost, and profits and losses from a particular voyage.

The introduction of the telegraph resulted in a more comprehensive coverage of shipping by the newspapers. The movements of vessels and their cargoes, accidents and shipwrecks were reported in far greater detail. More commercial shipping registers were being published and the older ones were expanded to include more information.

After Confederation, the registration of vessels and the general management of shipping was supervised by the Department of Marine and Fisheries. However, duplicate copies of the shipping registers and subsequent transactions were still sent to London. Annual reports first appeared in 1868, and the first "List of Vessels on the Registry Books of Canada" appeared in 1873 and 1874. Subsequent lists were issued every three years until 1901 when they were published annually.

Lists of certificates of competency and certificates of service granted to masters and mates, statements of wrecks and casualties, lists of lighthouses, buoys and markers, and general information on shipping all appear in the annual reports. Also included are statements of the number of new vessels built and the number of vessels on the registry books, with a breakdown by province.

This period saw the final development of the sailing ship with further improvements in design and rigging. The introduction of the double topgallant in 1872, the greater use of wire rigging and more deck fittings, all improved conditions on board and made the vessels more efficient. While there were many fast vessels and quick passages, most of the vessels were built for large carrying capacity.

By the mid-1880s, however, the wooden square-rigged sailing ship was rapidly becoming obsolete. Gradually, it was being replaced by the steel steamship, a more efficient and reliable method of transportation. In an attempt to compete with the steamship, a number of very large sailing vessels were built in order to carry greater cargoes. There was also a gradual adaptation of the fore-and-aft rig and the introduction of the barquentine and the three- and four-masted schooners. All of these required smaller crews, were more manoeuvreable and cost less to operate. For a number of years they attempted to hold their own against the steamers and actually saw a revival during World War I. A few merchants such as Troop, Thomson, Carmichael, Lovitt and others did purchase steel sailing vessels and steamships but most were not prepared to make the transition.

By the 1890s many of the builders and owners were old men, and few of the younger men were willing to continue the businesses. While the wooden sailing ship could be built with little overhead, a great deal of capital was needed to establish and outfit a yard for building steel vessels. Although steel vessels could carry large cargoes, they were more expensive to buy and required more capital to operate. The great profits of the earlier years were no longer to be made and most businesses preferred to put their money into more lucrative ventures.

Captain Hiram Coalfleet

Apart from shipwrecks along the coast, many disabled vessels had to be abandoned at sea. If the crew were fortunate they might be sighted by another vessel and taken off before their vessel sank. In many cases the lifeboats were smashed to pieces before they could be launched. Often the crews took to the lifeboats only to be drowned in the heavy seas.

There are many stories of rescues of the crews of disabled vessels. One of these concerns the rescue of the passengers and crew of the *Industry* of Halifax by the *Providence* of Windsor in 1868. The *Providence*, a barque of 478 tons, was built in 1867 by Ebenezer Bigelow and owned by the builder. The *Industry*, a schooner of 27 tons, was built in 1856 at Chester and owned by Roland B. Currie and Lewis Sponagle.

On December 11, 1868, the *Industry* left the La Have River for Halifax. On board were the master, a crew of three and two passengers, including a young girl of eighteen. Just off Sambro Island the vessel ran into stormy weather and was forced to run out to sea. For two weeks she attempted to ride out the storm but was severely damaged and the crew suffered from want of food and water.

On December 29 they were sighted by the *Providence*. A heavy sea was running and the wind was blowing a gale. The crew of the barque attempted to launch a boat but it was smashed to pieces and lost. Captain Hiram Coalfleet manoeuvred his vessel to windward of the schooner and, backing his topsails, slowly drifted down to the other vessel. When the two vessels touched, the captain's brother, Abel, lowered himself from the main yardarm onto the deck of the schooner and the woman and five men were pulled to safety.

For their bravery in accomplishing the rescue the Government of Canada presented Hiram Coalfleet with a gold watch, and his brother Abel with a pair of binoculars. The pair of binoculars has survived. The gold watch was lost on the wreck of the *Happy Home* in 1881.

The *Happy Home*, a barque of 884 tons, was built at Hantsport in 1874 by John Davison for the Churchill fleet. On January 3, 1881, while on a voyage from Hamburg to Saint John, the vessel struck Trinity Ledge off Port Maitland, Yarmouth County, filled with water and went over on her beam end. In an attempt to cut away the lifeboats, the cook was drowned. Captain Hiram Coalfleet, his wife, their eight-year-old daughter and twelve members of the crew were lashed to the rigging. Mrs. Coalfleet and the child died from exposure during the night and the others were rescued the following morning. It was Captain Coalfleet's last command. His legs were frozen and he was crippled for life.

The photograph on the right shows Captain Coalfleet on board the ship *Kilbrannan* prior to taking command of the *Providence*. In the back row, from left to right are: the ship's carpenter, Mrs. Hiram Coalfleet, Captain Hiram Coalfleet, Abel Coalfleet (the first mate), and the second mate. The child in the middle row is Rupert Coalfleet, son of the captain and his wife.

"KILBRANNAN"

The Robert Godfrey

In a severe storm at sea one of the greatest hazards for a sailing ship was to be dismasted. Unless prompt action was taken and the tons of broken masts, yards and rigging were quickly cut away, further damage would be done to the decks and planking, and the vessel might be swamped, or even capsize. This description of a dismasting is taken from the official Log[3] of the barque *Robert Godfrey* kept by the master, David Taylor. Taylor had on board his brother Matthew M. Taylor as second mate. The vessel sailed from Baltimore on January 6, 1869, laden with a cargo of Indian corn, rosin and bark.

> Jan. 20, 1869   Lat 42 23′N
> at 12:30 p.m.   Long 48 31′W
> Charles Brown O.S. was washed from the lee wheel overboard and lost by a sea that boarded the ship while scudding in a hurricane. John Maney A.B. who had the weather wheel was washed forward off the poop and was found in the water on the main deck with his knee dislocated, Matthew M. Taylor 2 mate and Frank Oulton A.B. was also washed forward of the poop and both injured Brusis etc. The same sea completely swept the poop of everything skylight companionway Binacle took away one half of the wheel with the remaining half we managed to steer her until we got in the fore topsail and foresail and then we hove to on starboard tack but the wind was blowing so very hard the ship laid almost on her beam ends and in about 4 hours after the first accident a sea hit the bowsprit and with the strain of the mast on it carried it away square with the knighthead and a few minutes more we cut the lanyards and the fore mast went at the deck and carried the mainmast away with the mizzen topmast (we had to cut away the lanyards and lost everything attached to them.)

Two weeks later more problems were encountered because some of the crew, exhausted from pumping, wished to abandon ship.

> Feb. 7, 1869   Lat 45 20′N
> 4 A.M.   Long 25 30′W
> At 4 A.M. John Kingsbury A.B. let the wheel spin (A trick he is in the habit of doing) and carried away the tiller block on the starboard side and consequently the ship came to and done considerable damage to sails and shipped a good deal of water it is believed he done this on purpose to disable the steering gear so we would be obliged to abandon ship he has also at several times been heard to say that it was no use pumping and might as well give up first as last. He will not be allowed to go to the wheel again while in the ship.

The barque arrived at Liverpool on February 20 under jury rig. A description of the damage to the vessel and the jury rig employed by David Taylor to bring the vessel into port is summarized in the surveyors' report[4] on March 2, 1869:

> . . . we found the Bowsprit carried away at the Knight heads, the fore & main masts gone below the coamings of the upper deck with all yards & rigging attached, the mizen mast alone being left. A steering sail boom was rigged for a Foremast and a Jibboom for a main mast to which different sails had been fitted. . . .

David Taylor received a cheque from the Maritime Insurance Company for £50 ". . . as a recognition of your extraordinary exertions & ability in successfully bringing your ship the *Robert Godfrey* into this port under jury mast. . . ."[5]

The *Robert Godfrey*, a barque of 773 tons, was launched from the yard of Robert Chapman at Rockland, New Brunswick, on May 25, 1868. She was the first large vessel to be built at the yard since its establishment in 1860. Oliver Pittfield came from Saint John to superintend the building of the *Robert Godfrey*, which cost, ready for sea, $24,781.44. She was owned by Robert Chapman and sixteen other people from the Dorchester area. On December 27, 1880, the vessel was wrecked on Cape Sans Vito, Sicily.

Chapman continued building until 1883 and in all constructed thirty-one vessels. His largest was the *S. B. Weldon*, a ship of 1530 tons built in 1878.

This watercolour shows the *Robert Godfrey* at anchor. The positions of the braces and standing rigging are clearly shown.

The Robert Godfrey

Barque   773 Tons
Built in 1868 at Rockland, N.B.,
by Robert Chapman.
158.4′ x 34.6′ x 20.25′

Watercolour.
Unsigned and undated.
Courtesy of Mr. Alfred Taylor,
Taylor Village, N.B.

The Orion

Despite the financial crash of the Joseph Cunard empire in 1848, and the slump that followed, this period ushered in the great ship-building era of the Miramichi. Joseph Russell continued to build at Beaubears Island. James Johnson and John Mackie, who had joined partnership in 1845, took over the Cunard shipyard and in 1849 built the *Sir Edmund Head*, a ship of 624 tons.

In 1855 William Muirhead built his first vessel, the *Northern Bride*, a ship of 853 tons. Ten years later he built the *Royal Arch*, a ship of 1623 tons, the largest vessel to be built in northern New Brunswick.

The firm of Gilmore, Rankin & Company, a branch of Pollock, Gilmore & Company of Glasgow, had been established at Douglastown in 1812 and soon became major ship owners. However, it was not until 1857 that they operated their own yard. Other builders included Harley & Burchill, John Haws, Peter Mitchell, William & Robert Johnston and James Henderson.

The *Orion*, a schooner of 95 tons, was built by James Henderson in 1869. She was registered at Miramichi on July 14, 1869, and owned by A. Ernest Hutchinson. The vessel had a short life. She was wrecked on Seven Islands in the St. Lawrence River in the fall of 1869.

The spar plan of the *Orion* is shown on the right. She represents one of the many hundreds of schooners built in the Maritimes during this period.

Orion
DIMENSIONS OF SPARS
(in feet)

Spar	Fore	Main
Mast — deck to truck	96	98
Lower mast — deck to cap	67	69
Topmast	35	35
Boom	25	58
Gaff	26	27.6
Jib-boom	34	

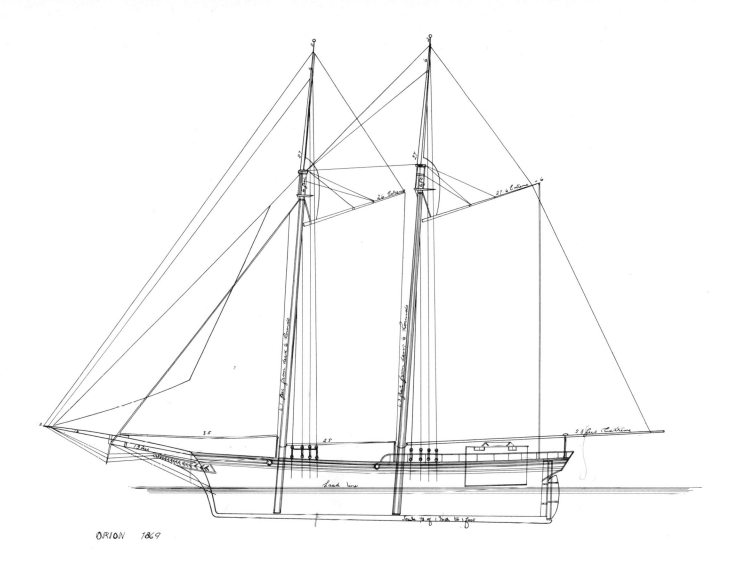

ORION 1869

The Orion

Schooner   95 Tons
Built in 1869 at Douglastown, N.B.,
by James Henderson.
78.4′ x 21.9′ x 8.1′

Original spar plan: courtesy
of the New Brunswick Museum,
Saint John, N.B.
Traced by Thomas Lackey and
B. Renton Goodwyn, Halifax, N.S.

105

Shelburne, Nova Scotia

After Shelburne closed as a port of registry in 1823 all vessels were registered at Halifax until 1840, when many were registered at Liverpool and Yarmouth. Shelburne reopened as a port of registry in 1858 but many of the larger vessels continued to be registered at Halifax and Yarmouth.

One of the first prominent builders of Shelburne was William Muir, who began in 1827 when he launched the *Olinda*, a brig of 126 tons. Muir continued building until the 1860s. Other members of the Muir family who were building during this period were James, Samuel and Thomas. Other builders included John Cox, George Cox, Charles Cox and John Dexter at Shelburne, James D. Coffin at Clyde River, Warren Doane at Barrington, Charles A. Holden at Jordan River and Joseph F. Freeman and James Dexter at Sable River.

Most of the vessels built at Shelburne and vicinity were small schooners and brigantines and all were locally owned. However, by the early 1860s a number of barques had been launched, and in 1877 the *Commerce*, a ship of 1297 tons, was built at Shelburne

by Brown and Pentz for Lindley M. M. Willet. On September 26, 1878, while on a voyage from Philadelphia to Antwerp with a cargo of 64,452 bushels of wheat valued at $75,197, she was run into and sunk by the S.S. *Empusa*, and two of her crew were drowned.

The *Autocrat*, a barque of 665 tons, was built at Shelburne in 1870 by P. Young. The vessel was registered at Yarmouth on October 27 and owned by John W. Moody (who was the managing owner), Augustus F. Stoneman, Joseph W. McMullen, Freeman Gardner and John Flint — all shipowners of Yarmouth. On March 24, 1887, she was sold to Norwegian subjects and was still afloat ten years later.

This painting shows the *Autocrat* "hove down" in a gale of wind in February 1884. The vessel is shipping a great deal of water and the inner jib has been completely blown out of the ropes. The spanker gaff is broken and the men are letting go the peak halliard and topping lift so that the sail can be furled. All other sails are furled except the main lower topsail which is goose-winged. The weather-half of the sail has been furled leaving only a small portion of the sail drawing.

"Autocrat" hove down in a gale of Wind. February 1884

The Autocrat

Barque   665 Tons
Built in 1870 at Shelburne, N.S.,
by P. Young.
152.0′ x 32.6′ x 20.4′

Oil on canvas.
By Edward Adam, 1884.
Courtesy of the Nova Scotia
Museum, Halifax, N.S.

The Adriatic

The *Adriatic*, a barque of 436 tons, was built by J. R. McKay at New Glasgow and registered at Pictou on July 21, 1870. The managing owner was John Turner Ives, a merchant of Pictou. Just over two months later, the barque was back in Pictou Harbour in a semiderelict condition and the master, John Duncan Mac-Kenzie, appeared before John D. McLeod, Notary Public, to enter his protest[6] against the vessel.

> . . . sailed on the evening of the fifteenth day of September last from Fall River in the State of Massacheusetts for Pictou in ballast the said Barque being then tight staunch strong and well manned and arrived in the said port of Pictou this first day of October and having encountered severe gales and tempestuous seas and the said barque having sustained great damage and injury on the passage, . . .

The extent of the damage to the vessel is given in the following surveyor's report[7] signed by William Crevar and Donald Cameron, shipmasters, and Daniel MacDonald, master shipbuilder, all of Pictou.

> . . . we found her jibboom and all the gear attached to it gone, martingale and whiskers and all the gear attached also gone, foremast badly chafed in consequence of foretopsail yard being broken and chafing across it, foretopsail Yards Upper and lower with topgallant and Royal Yards all gone with the standing and running gear attached, Foretopmasts, topgallants and Royal masts and all the gear attached gone, Upper maintopsail Yard with topgallant Yard and Royal and all standing and running gear attached gone (with the exception of topmast backstays and some damaged rigging). Mizzen topmast broken about seven feet above the cap and all gear belonging to it cut, bent and chafed, Spanker gaff broken, Foretopmast staysail jib and flying jib, Upper and Lower topsail and Royal, Main Royal and maintopgallant sails all gone, lower and Upper Main topsails and mizzen topmast staysail much chaffed and holes worn in several places by the wreck of spars, foresail chafed throughout and holes in several places. Mainsail also damaged and holes worn in several places, and much damaged with iron rust, fore, main and mizzen shrouds badly chafed, Side lights broken stern of boat broken and otherwise badly damaged and having examined the Log Book of the said barque and finding therefrom that her spars were dragging under her bottom and judging therefrom that she may have sustained other injuries thereby and also finding that the said Barque was for a time while at sea on her beam ends and would thereby be strained we therefore
>
> Order or recommend
>
> That the said Barque be hauled on the Marine Slip at Pictou with a view to a further examination of her as regards the condition of her bottom, that all the Masts, Spars, Rigging and Apparel of the said Barque so lost or damaged and injured as aforesaid be replaced by and with new materials, and that in respect of the aforesaid and consequent injuries and the said Barque be thoroughly and fully repaired. . . .

The *Adriatic* was thoroughly repaired and continued trading. She was sold in London on September 6, 1875, to Norwegian subjects and was still operating in the late 1880s.

This painting shows the *Adriatic* under full sail. The vessel's signal letters, J.V.T.H., have been hoisted at the mizzen truck.

The Adriatic

Barque   436 Tons
Built in 1870 at New Glasgow, N.S.,
by J. R. McKay.
141.6′ x 31.8′ x 12.9′

Oil on canvas.
By Edward Adam, undated.
Courtesy of the Nova Scotia
Museum, Halifax, N.S.

The Abram Young

Born in 1808 at Upper Granville, Nova Scotia, Jacob Valentine Troop moved his family to Saint John in 1840. In 1847 he purchased a half share in the *Kate*, a schooner of 60 tons. Later that year the *Emily*, a brigantine of 116 tons, was built for him by Abram Young of Granville. Gradually the number of vessels owned by Troop increased and he soon became a prominent merchant and owned one of the largest fleets of vessels operating out of Saint John. He maintained a very high standard and employed the best masters he could get. He kept his vessels well equipped and in good order.

By the late 1860s he was joined by his son, Howard D. Troop, who took over the business. The company continued to prosper and was the first in Saint John to own steel sailing vessels. Jacob V. Troop died in 1881, and on the death of his son Howard in 1912 the company closed.

The Troops engaged a number of shipbuilders including Abram Young at Granville, John S. Parker at Tynemouth Creek and David Lynch at Portland, New Brunswick. From 1841 until 1878, the year before his death, Abram Young built a number of vessels for the Troop fleet. One of these was the *Abram Young*, a barque of 756 tons, built at Granville, and launched on August 27, 1870. The vessel remained in the Troop fleet until sold in 1890, when she was transferred to Norwegian ownership and renamed *Ferda*. She was still afloat in 1901.

The painting shows the *Abram Young* in a severe storm with all her lower sails blown away except the spanker and outer jibs which are furled. She is being swept by heavy seas. The inverted Red Ensign has been hoisted at the mizzen topmast and the signal letters "N.C." have been hoisted in the port mizzen shrouds. Both are signals of distress. A steamer can be seen off her starboard bow. According to family tradition, the *Abram Young* had also lost her rudder and the steamer ignored their distress signals. However, William F. Palmer, the master, was able to ship a jury rudder and make port. He also managed to get the name of the steamer and reported her to the authorities. The steamer's captain and owners were fined for not standing by a vessel in distress. Unfortunately, it has not been possible to date this incident.

The Abram Young

Barque   756 Tons
Built in 1870 at Granville, N.S.,
by Abram Young.
154.8′ x 33.9′ x 20.0′

Oil on canvas.
Unsigned and undated.
Courtesy of Mr. Percy Palmer,
Moncton, N.B.

The Jardine Brothers

Barque   523 Tons
Built in 1870 at Richibucto, N.B.,
by John and Thomas Jardine.
145.5′ x 30.3′ x 17.1′

Oil on canvas.
By W. H. York, 1880.
Courtesy of the New Brunswick
Museum, Saint John, N.B.

The Jardine Brothers

The Jardines of Richibucto are another example of a family who dominated shipbuilding over a long period of time. When Robert and John Jardine joined partnership in 1824, it was to be the start of a family business that over the next sixty years constructed more than eighty vessels. Their first vessel was the *Helen Douglas*, a brig of 237 tons built by Walter Neilson in 1825. Six more vessels were built for them by various master builders before the partnership dissolved in 1831 and John continued on his own. From 1833 until 1847 he constructed more than thirty vessels, an average of nearly two a year. Nearly all were ships and barques of 400 to 700 tons, built for immediate sale in England.

In the meantime, John and Thomas Jardine, nephews of John Jardine Sr., had arrived from Scotland to work in their uncle's yard. Thomas Jardine is listed as the builder of a couple of small brigs as early as 1843 and eventually he and his brother Thomas established their own yard. In 1850 they launched their first vessel, the *Lochmaden Castle*, a ship of 1012 tons, and continued in operation for another thirty-four years. For many years they built for David Jardine (a son of John Jardine Sr.), who had gone to Liverpool, England, and established the firm of Farnsworth and Jardine, shipowners and timber merchants.

On June 11, 1870, John and Thomas Jardine launched the *Jardine Brothers*, a barque of 523 tons. She was the first of their vessels that they owned and operated on their own. From then until 1884 they built almost entirely for themselves and only a few were sent to Liverpool. When, in 1884, they built their last vessel, the *Valona*, a barque of 799 tons, they had constructed over forty-five ships and barques. With the exception of a few which were sent over on a Governor's Pass, all were registered at Miramichi until Richibucto opened as a port of registry in 1880.

The *Jardine Brothers* was owned by John and Thomas Jardine for twelve years. On August 11, 1882, the *Daily Sun* of Saint John, New Brunswick, reported:

Wrecked — Messrs D. & J. Ritchie & Co. Newcastle received a despatch on Tuesday last from the captain of the bark "Jardine Brothers" stating that that vessel was a total wreck at St. Pierre. The vessel was bound from Liverpool to Newcastle and had a part cargo, consisting of about 180 Tons of salt. The cargo is covered by insurance and the vessel partly so. Chatham Advance.

This dramatic painting shows the *Jardine Brothers* running in heavy weather under her main lower topsail. All other sails have been carefully furled. The spanker is furled against a trysail mast, set abaft the mizzen.

The Harriet Campbell

Barque   649 Tons
Built in 1873 at Weymouth, N.S.,
by Colin Campbell.
148.0′ x 31.5′ x 19.2′

Oil on canvas.
By W. H. York, 1884.
Courtesy of the New Brunswick
Museum, Saint John, N.B.

Colin Campbell

Like many Maritime merchants in the nineteenth century, Colin Campbell of Weymouth, Nova Scotia, ran a general store, carried on an extensive timber trade and built and operated his own vessels. Campbell began as a shipowner in 1848 and a number of vessels were built for him at Weymouth. Later, in 1867, he operated his own yard next to his new home, "Beechwood," at Weymouth North, and continued building and operating a fleet of vessels until his death in 1881. During this period he built ten barques, the largest being the *Campbell*, of 1132 tons, launched in 1879. All were named for members of his family. His sons helped with the business at home, and one son, John, became the company agent in London.

The *Harriet Campbell*, a barque of 649 tons, was built in 1873 and named after John's wife. The vessel was registered at Digby and owned by Colin Campbell and his son Gordon. After Colin's death the vessel was owned by various members of the Campbell family and finally, in August 1885, was sold to Solomon and George Edgett of St. John's, Newfoundland, and owned by them until abandoned at sea in Lat 31°–10″N Long 45°W on May 30, 1889.

Fortunately, the records of both Colin Campbell and his son Gordon D. Campbell have survived. The ledgers[8] give detailed builders' costs as well as operating costs of most of the Campbell vessels. The total cost of the *Harriet Campbell* was $30,872.33. The men's wages ranged from 75 cents to $1.25 per day. A number of items of interest from the ledgers are listed below.

To model and moulds (made from last ship)	$ 45.00
Cutting & Moulding Timber at Camp	1,007.00
1 Mizzen mast from E. Dexter	36.00

15,356 Treenails	139.60
1 Bowsprit E. Dexter	25.00
Fore and Main Mast Geo. E. Young	325.00
Bill of Iron Knees	1,393.00
1 Figure head (billet) black & gilt	12.00
Charles R. Middleton bill for making sails	230.47
Chronometer	120.00
Clock	5.00
Binnacle & Compass, Pat Log, Deep Sea Lead & Lines	54.78
Anchors obtained from London & Boston	
Dartmouth Ropework Co.	1,333.91
Horton & Lewis bill of Blocks	387.80
A. Potters Bill ironwork bending Knees	911.16
William Lyons Job joinering 1 per ton	675.00
John Smith Sparmaker	221.00
Sparmaker board 15 weeks at $2½	37.50
Morris Titus bill of Cabin furniture	26.50
Alex Sims Classification fee	
(Bureau Veritas)	184.94
Ed Everitts Classification fee	
(American Lloyds)	37.00
Edward Everett surveying fee for	
American Lloyds	35.00
Amount of labour rend off time book including	
Calking Rigging & C	9,020.32
Total cost of planks	
(exc of what came from C.C. & Co)	639.15

This painting of the *Harriet Campbell* by W. H. York, dated Liverpool 1884, shows the vessel under full sail entering harbour. The vessel wears the Campbell house flag at the main truck and the Canadian Red Ensign at the spanker gaff. The barque's signal letters, W.B.H.C., have been hoisted at the mizzen truck and the pilot jack at the fore truck.

Mutiny on the Lennie

In the fall of 1875 the *Lennie*, a ship of 984 tons, became famous because of a mutiny and the brutal murder of her captain and two mates. The vessel was built in 1871 at Belleveau's Cove by R. Bellevue and owned by William D. Lovitt, a major shipowner of Yarmouth, Nova Scotia.

The *Lennie* sailed from Antwerp in ballast on October 23, 1875, for Sandy Hook for orders. On board were Captain Stanley Hatfield of Yarmouth, master; Joseph Wortley of Belfast, first mate; Richard McDonald of Saint John, New Brunswick, second mate; Constant Van Hoydonck of Belgium, steward; and Henry Trousselot, a sixteen-year-old from Denmark, who was cabin boy. The remaining eleven men were ABs and included four Greeks, three Turks, an Austrian, an Italian, a Dane and an Englishman.

In the early morning of October 31, the vessel was still in the English Channel. When the watch was changed at 4 A.M. and all hands were on deck, the captain gave orders to tack the ship. When the vessel came about, the braces got fouled and the captain upbraided the crew for their poor handling of the yards. Without warning, one of the Greek sailors attacked the Captain with a knife and, after a short struggle, killed him. The second mate rushed to the captain's assistance and was also stabbed by the Greek. When the first mate, who was aloft on one of the yards, reached the deck, he was killed by the cook. The bodies of all three men were weighted and thrown overboard. During the fight the Belgian steward, Constant Van Hoydonck, who was below at the time, attempted to get on deck but was locked in his cabin.

As in the case of the famous *Saladin* mutiny in 1844, the crew were left in command of a vessel they could not handle. They proposed that Van Hoydonck, who knew navigation, take the ship to Greece. The steward, feigning agreement, promptly set a course for the Bristol Channel but later was forced to change course and headed for the French coast.

Several times the crew became suspicious of his activities and relieved him of command, only to reinstate him when they realized they could not handle the vessel themselves. Eventually the vessel was anchored off the Ile de Ré on the coast of France. In the meantime, Van Hoydonck and the cabin boy spent their time writing appeals for help in French and English, stuffing them into bottles and throwing them overboard.

On November 9, while still at anchor off Ile de Ré, six of the ringleaders demanded to know the nature of the country. Van Hoydonck blandly told them it was a republic with no police, and the six subsequently departed for shore. The next morning Van Hoydonck hoisted a distress signal and shortly afterwards a French gunboat came alongside the *Lennie* and took charge. A few days later the six deserters were arrested.

The trial took place in London. Four of the six men were sentenced to death and executed. With the salvage money he received from the owners of the *Lennie*, Van Hoydonck retired and opened a tavern in London.

Four years after the mutiny, the rig of the *Lennie* was changed to that of a barque and the vessel remained in the Lovitt fleet for another thirteen years. On May 2, 1892, she was sold to be used as a hulk at Cork, Ireland.

The vessel is shown in this watercolour entering harbour. The cross-jack and the royals are being clewed up. The Lovitt house flag is being worn at the mainmast. The schooner off the starboard bow is probably the pilot boat.

The Lennie

Ship   984 Tons
Built in 1871 at Belleveau's Cove, N.S.,
by R. Bellevue.
175.0' x 35.0' x 22.0'

The Talisman

By the early 1860s the double topsail had been introduced on nearly all large vessels. This not only facilitated the furling and handling of the large topsails but also required a smaller crew since much of the work could be done from the deck. This modification was extended to the topgallant sail in 1872.

The topgallant sail was split horizontally into two sails, an upper topgallant and a lower topgallant, each on its own yard. The lower topgallant yard was secured to the topmast cap and did not move up and down. The upper topgallant yard was raised into position when the sail was set and lowered when the sail was furled.

The double topgallant rig is shown clearly in this painting of the *Talisman*, one of the first Maritime vessels to adopt the new rig. She is shown passing Heligoland signalling for a pilot. Her master was Captain A. Baker. The vessel wears the Dennis and Doane house flag and her signal letters, L.M.B.K., have been hoisted at the mizzen.

The new rig, however, does not appear to have been widely used, since many large vessels built after this date did not adopt the alteration. The ship, *William D. Lawrence*, built two years later at Maitland and the largest vessel constructed in the Maritimes, still carried only single topgallants.

The *Talisman*, a barque of 953 tons, was built by George Jenkins at Beaver River in 1872, was registered at Yarmouth and owned by Freeman Dennis, George B. Doane and a number of other merchants. In 1881 she was owned and operated by Jacob Bingay of Yarmouth and in 1888 by her master, Albert Baker. A year later the vessel was sold to John Starr DeWolf of Liverpool, England, but was not transferred to Liverpool until 1894. In December of the next year she was lost on the Dutch coast with all hands.

The Talisman

Barque   953 Tons
Built in 1872 at Beaver River, N.S.,
by George Jenkins.
173.7' x 36.2' x 21.6'

Oil on canvas.
By H. Petersen and P. C. Holm.
Courtesy of Mrs. Gerald Lowe,
Amherst, N.S.

The Royal Harrie

Shipbuilding began at Hopewell, New Brunswick, in the early part of the nineteenth century. Two of the earliest vessels were the *Betsey*, a schooner of 49 tons built in 1803 and the *Lily*, a schooner of 72 tons built in 1807. During the 1820s and 1830s the number steadily increased, and builders included John Calhoon, James Brewster and George Rogers. In 1825 Samuel Clark built the *Mersey*, a brig of 316 tons, and in 1828 James Whitney built the *Navarino*, a barque of 333 tons. These were probably the first of their type built in the area.

From 1828 until the late nineteenth century, various members of the Bennett family were involved in shipbuilding: William, Nathan, Nehemiah and Joel. In 1847 William Bennett built the *Elizabeth Bentley*, a ship of 867 tons. She was one of a number of vessels built by the Bennetts at Hopewell and Hillsborough for Nathan DeMill of Saint John.

Two of the early vessels built at Hillsborough were the *Mary and Eliza*, a schooner of 61 tons built in 1818, and the *Triumph*, a schooner of 26 tons built in 1822. One of the first large vessels was the *Refuge*, a ship of 825 tons built in 1850 by William Bennett.

Another prominent New Brunswick builder who began in Hillsborough was William Hickman. Born in 1823, Hickman built three vessels at Hillsborough between 1863 and 1865 before moving to Dorchester and establishing his shipyard on Dorchester Island. His largest vessel built at Hillsborough was the *Fanny Atkinson*, a barque of 626 tons launched in 1865. From 1867 until 1882 Hickman built eighteen vessels at Dorchester including three ships, thirteen barques, a brigantine and a schooner. His largest vessel, the *Charlie Hickman*, a ship of 1543 tons, was launched in 1871.

In 1868 Hickman built the *Maggie Chapman*, a barque of 780 tons. On October 15, two days before the launching, Robert Chapman, Hickman's bitter rival across the river, wrote to David Taylor, master of the *Robert Godfrey*:

> . . . Rutherford is to take charge of Hickmans new Bark until Hans Atkinson gets out and then is to take the Fanny but from what he learned since he came home he is sick of his bargain as it is generally understood here that she leaks like a basket notwithstanding she was caulked all over last year and besides is now just as bare as possible. I guess there is no doubt she is a perfect trap and always was though they blowed about her so much and I am satisfied even the one he Hickman has just built is very little better though they blow great on her as out of 50 or 60 men working on her he has never had over 8 or 10 Good men and the Foreman is not the man either. . . .[9]

In spite of Chapman's sarcastic remarks about the quality of workmanship on the *Maggie Chapman*, the vessel remained in the Hickman fleet for ten years. The *Fanny Atkinson*, in fact, outlasted the *Robert Godfrey*, Chapman's new vessel, launched several months before.

The first New Brunswick-built barquentine to be registered at Saint John was the *Royal Harrie* of 482 tons, built at Hopewell in 1872 by John Leander Pye. The vessel was owned by John and Simon Leonard and other merchants of Saint John. She was condemned and sold at Saint Helena on March 25, 1884.

This watercolour shows clearly the barquentine rig which became popular at this time. She is square-rigged on the foremast and fore-and-aft-rigged on the main and mizzen.

The Royal Harrie

Barquentine   482 Tons
Built in 1872 at Hopewell, N.B.,
by J. L. Pye.
137.7′ x 32.0′ x 16.9′

Watercolour.
By Edward J. Russell, undated.
Courtesy of the New Brunswick
Museum, Saint John, N.B.

Memoranda

In port at Darien, Ga. 29th ult, barque *Sheffield*, Sloan, and brig *Magdala*. Upham, for this port; and barque *Morocco*, Farnsworth, for the United Kingdom.

Off the South Stack, Jan'y 9th, ship *Charles Bal* from Liverpool for Rangoon.

Passed through Hell Gate, 2d inst, schooner *Alba*, Crowley, hence for New York.

Schr *Emma W Day*, from Boston. ef and for Pembroke, went ashore on West Quoddy Bay, 25th ult, but came off next morning, sustaining but little damage.

Barque *Harriet*, Tyrell, from Quebec for Queenstown, which put into St Johns, Nfl t. last fall in distress, cleared 19th ult to resume her voyage, having repaired.

In port at Newcastle. (Del) 2d inst, barque *Silver Cloud*, Taylor, from Philadelphia for this port; and brig *Attie Durkee*, Rogers, from Philadelphia for Cienfuegos, detained by ice.

In port at Newport, 4th inst, schooner *Statesman*, Cole, for Shulee, NS.

In port at Mayaguez, PR, 17th ult, ship *Lord of the Seas*, for Inagua, to load salt for Halifax, NS.

Off Deal, 8th inst, ship *Kate Troop*, Crocker, from Savannah for Amsterdam.

Schr *H K White*, (of Boston) Finley, St John, NB, for New York, reports 3d inst, off Cape Cod, in a gale from the eastward. lost fore-topmast, jib. boom and boat; also split foresail and j b. Anchored off Nauset 4th, and lost part of deck load of lumber.

Brig *Aurora*, Fraser, at Barbados 21st ult, from Liverpo l. NS, had heavy weather on the passage and lost part of deck load.

Schr *Annie Bayard*, Whelpley, at Barbados, 13th ult, from Norfolk, lost part of deck load on the passage, having encountered heavy weather.

In port at Demerara, 23d ult, barque *Norma*, Chapman, from Glasgow—arrived 8th ult.

Returned to Halifax, 8th inst, schrs *Juliet*, Simpson, for this port; and *Sappho*, Spragg, for Portland—both sailed same day.

Barque *Helen Campbell*, Brooks, from Boston Jan 1st. or London, put into Cardy, Wales, 1st inst, leaky.

Barque *Manitoba*, Durkee, before reported wrecked off Penzance, and one of the crew drowned, was from Havre for Bristol Channel for orders. Capt D was among the saved.

Barque *Lydia*, Scoville, from Antwerp for Philadelphia, remained at St Thomas 30th ult. Had discharged and was undergoing repairs.

Ship *Elizabeth Fry*, Meikle, from New Orleans for Liverpool, with 3100 bales cotton, was burned to the water's edge 5th inst, 200 miles S by E from Savannah. The captain and crew were picked up on the 6th, by barque *Circassian*, from Rio Janeiro, which landed them at Savannah 7th. The E. F. was 1094 tons register, built at Moncton, N B, in 1861, and hailed from Liverpool.

Barque *Lydia*, Scoville, from Antwerp for Philadelphia, remained at St Thomas 30th ult: had discharged and was undergoing repairs.

Notice to Mariners.

The Can Buoy at Wood's Hole, has changed its position, the ice crowded it over on the north side of the channel. Vessels will pass to the south of the buoy instead of the north as before.

Revenue cutter *Active* reports the Nun Boy from Quicks Hole about a mile south of its proper place.

BOSTON, Feb'y 9th.—The Shovelful and Handkerchief Light Vessels, recently moved a short distance by the ice, have been restored to their proper positions.

By order of the Lighthouse Board.

Spoken.

Dec 10th, lat 12.24 S, lon 31.12 W, barque, *Gipsy*, Cremor, from Boston. for Monte Video.

Dec 26th, lat 2 S, lon 29 W, ship *Eurydice*, of this port.

Jan'y 15th, lat 49, lon 18 51. ship *Andrew Lovitt*, Perry, from Philadelphia for Bremen.

January 15th, lat 49 N, lon 29 W, barque *Kentville*, Doyle, from Baker's Island for Queenstown.

Jan. 20th, lat 22.29, lon 59 21 schr *Mocking Bird*, lumber laden, bound South.

Feb'y 3d, lat 39.20, lon 65 31, brig *Mabel*, from this port for Havana.

Disasters:

Captain Lothrop, of brig *Thames*, of Five Islands, NS. before reported abandoned and crew taken to New York by the steamer *Tillie*. reports left Abaco, Bahamas January 24th, with a cargo of phosphate, for Hampton Roads for orders. On 27th had a furious gale from the S; between 3 and 4 o'clock AM. 28th, was struck by a heavy sea; heard a rushing of water in the run; took up the scuttle in the cabin; found five feet of water. On examination found the whole stern work started and impossible to stop the leak; kept her afloat by pumping and bailing until 4 o'clock PM same day, then commenced throwing out cargo to lighten ship. 29th, found ourselves on the western edge of the Gulf Stream. The cargo becoming wet, the crew worn out with constant exertion and great exposure, and no possible chance to save the brig, concluded to abandon her. Sighting a steamer, raised a signal of distress: she bore down upon us, and proved to be the *Tillie*, Capt Deering from Havana for New York, and at 10 o'clock AM, Jan'y 29th, abandoned the brig in a sinking condition, with six feet of water in the hold, and a heavy gale blowing at the time. We were taken on board the steamer and brought to New York. Captain L has arrived in this city, and wishes to return his thanks to Captain Deering for his courtesy while on board the steamer.—*Boston Advertiser*, Feb'y 3d.

MACHIAS, Feb'y 6th.—The schr *Emma*, ashore at Moosepeck Ledge—bilged—full of water.

Schr *Lamartine*. ef and from Yarmouth, NS, for this port, went ashore at False Head, 28th ult, and became a total wreck.

The Weekly Telegraph,
Saint John, N.B.,
February 14, 1872.

The Author's Collection

The Weekly Telegraph

After the introduction of the telegraph system in the 1860s more extensive information was published in the local newspapers on the movement of shipping. Apart from the usual list of vessels that had entered and cleared the home port, reports began to be received from other British and foreign ports.

This column appeared in the *Weekly Telegraph* of Saint John, New Brunswick, on February 14, 1872. The "Notice to Mariners" gives details on the position of markers and buoys published by order of the Lighthouse Board. Underneath is a list of vessels "Spoken" by other vessels while at sea.

Under "Disasters," brief reports appear on shipwrecks, collisions and fires. In the "Memoranda" section, reports on the arrivals and departures of vessels at other ports are published as well as cargoes, accidents, etc. It is from these reports that it is possible, in many instances, to reconstruct the voyages and mishaps of a particular vessel.

Timber Ships

This photograph shows clearly the standard method of loading timber into wooden sailing ships. Tackles, running to the winches on the deck, are being used to load square timber into the hold through the bow ports. In order that the vessel may take up less space at the wharf, the jib-boom has been taken in and lies directly over the bowsprit. A sail is being used as an awning and an anchor is secured to the cathead.

Timber Ships at Quebec, 1872

Courtesy of the Notman Photographic
Archives, McCord Museum of McGill
University, Montreal, P.Q.

The William Owen

Prince Edward Island reached its last great peak of shipbuilding in 1874. An indication of the types of new vessels being built on the Island in that year is shown in the table below.

New Vessels built in Prince Edward Island in 1874
and registered at Charlottetown[10]

	Tons
22 Barks	10,878
3 Barquentines	1,093
14 Brigs	3,708
35 Brigantines	7,386
13 Schooners	1,420
1 Steamer	149
88 Vessels	24,634

Also in 1874 the *Star of the Isle*, a barquentine of 305 tons, was built by William T. Ellis at Bideford for James K. Scott and Robert Cock of Appledore. She was sent to Great Britain on a Governor's Pass to be registered at Bideford, England. The largest vessel built on the Island in this year was the *Lady Dufferin*, a barque of 920 tons, built by Donald Ramsay at Port Hill for James Yeo.

The *William Owen*, a barque of 599 tons, was one of eight new vessels built for Lemuel Cambridge Owen in 1874. She was launched on November 9 from the shipyard of John MacDougall at Dundas and owned jointly by Owen and William Welsh. The vessel remained on the Charlottetown register until January, 1889 when she was sold to Norwegians and renamed *William*.

The vessel is shown "hove to" on the starboard tack under jib and fore lower topsail with the main lower topsail backed. A boat has been launched and is going to the aid of a brig to leeward, which is presumably in distress. Unfortunately, the painting is not dated and it has not been possible to find out the incident which it depicts. The signal letters assigned to the vessel were W.M.S.F. However, the artist has mistakenly reversed the last two letters and the signal reads W.M.F.S.

The William Owen

Barque   599 Tons
Built in 1874 at Dundas, P.E.I.,
by John MacDougall.
160.0′ x 31.7′ x 17.9′

Oil on canvas.
Unsigned and undated.
Courtesy of the Prince Edward
Island Heritage Foundation,
Charlottetown, P.E.I.

The William D. Lawrence

The first vessel usually attributed to William D. Lawrence is the *St. Lawrence*, a brigantine of 170 tons, which he built in 1852 with his brother James. However, Lawrence had previously designed the *Wanderer*, a barque of 568 tons, while he was an apprentice in the yard of John Chappell, a shipbuilder in Dartmouth. The barque was built in 1849 for the firm of Fairbanks & Allison.

Between 1855 and 1863 Lawrence built four barques and a brigantine and in 1867 he launched the *Pegasus*, a ship of 1120 tons. This vessel was owned by Lawrence and his son-in-law, James Ellis, who was also the master.

On October 1, 1870, Lawrence wrote to Ellis:

> . . . Now in regards to the building of a new Ship, I beg to say:—that I have got one laid down in the mould loft all ready to make the moulds for, but will not commence to do any thing in the yard until I get means to go on in Safety. . . .
>
> The Ship that I have laid down in the mould loft is of the moddle of the PEGASUS. I have raised on her and cleaned of her Bow a little more, and made a new scale to make her larger, this model as it is now looks most splendid, and every boddy that has seen it, admires it. Dimentions as follows:— Length of Keel 220 feet, Beam moulded 46 feet, depth of hold 28 ft. 6 in., Rise of floor 18 inches in 36 feet, 8 inches more dead rise than the PEGASUS has. Please let me know what the prospect is for guano freights continuing hereafter; for if there is a prospect ahead, it will be encouraging in regard to building the New Ship.[11]

Construction of the new vessel, however, did not start until the fall of 1872. Two years later, on October 27, 1874, the *William D. Lawrence*, a ship of 2458 tons, was launched at Maitland, Nova Scotia.

Lawrence's accounts[12] show that the ship cost $107,452.98. She required 15,274 man days of work and the men's wages ranged from 90 cents to $1.60 per day. Lawrence's brother, Lockhart, who was the master builder, was paid between $2.00 and $2.50 per day. Lawrence's bill for his own time amounted to 500 days at $4.00 per day. The sails were made by Thomas Forhan of Halifax and cost $1,052.98.

The *William D. Lawrence* was owned by the builder and James Ellis until 1883 when she was sold on April 12 to Norwegian owners for £6,500. In a letter to the *Nova Scotian*, printed on January 12, 1884, Lawrence gave an account of the profits of the ship while under his ownership.

Cash paid on vessel	$ 80,000.00
Debt on vessel	27,452.00
Total cost	107,452.00
Expenses	150,445.00
Total cost of ship and expenses	257,897.00
Earning and sale of ship	398,945.00
Balance in favour of ship	140,848.00

This represents 22 per cent profit on the Initial investment of $80,000 over eight years.

On transfer to Norwegian owners, the ship's name was changed to *Kommander Svend Foyn* and she remained afloat for another fifteen years.

While the *William D. Lawrence* was the largest ship built in the Maritimes, she was in fact only slightly larger than the *Morning Light* built by William and Richard Wright in Saint John in 1855. Contrary to popular belief, she was not the largest square-rigged vessel built in British North America. The largest was the *Baron of Renfrew* of 5294 tons built by Charles Wood on the Island of Orleans, Quebec, in 1825. Her dimensions were: length, 304 feet 1 inch; breadth, 61 feet; depth of hold, 34 feet 9 inches. The second largest was the *Columbus* of 3690 tons built by Charles Wood in 1824. Her dimensions were: length, 301 feet 6 inches; breadth, 50 feet 7 inches; depth of hold, 29 feet 4 inches. Both vessels were rigged as four-masted barques.

The *William D. Lawrence* is shown in this painting with all sails set. Despite her size, she did not carry double topgallants. The sails above the royals are skysails and the vessel would be known as a three skysail yarder. The ship's signal letters, N.Q.D.C., are hoisted inferior to the Canadian Red Ensign which is being worn at the monkey gaff.

The William D. Lawrence

Ship   2458 Tons
Built in 1874 at Maitland, N.S.,
by William D. Lawrence.
262.0′ x 48.0′ x 29.1′

Oil on canvas.
Unsigned and undated.
Courtesy of the Nova Scotia
Museum, Halifax, N.S.

The Aneroid

One of the thirty-five brigantines launched in 1874 was the *Aneroid* of 229 tons built at West Point, Prince Edward Island, by Daniel C. Ramsay for John Lefurgey of Summerside. The vessel was registered at Charlottetown on June 9, 1874, and six months later sold to Thomas Browning Power and registered at Swansea, Wales.

This painting shows the *Aneroid* under full sail. Her signal letters, W.S.Q.G., have been hoisted inferior to the Red Ensign being worn at the spanker gaff. She carries a spanker and gaff topsail on the main. The gaff topsail appears to have been unusual in vessels built in the Maritimes and may have been fitted after she was sold in England. In 1891 the *Aneroid* was owned by Thomas H. Franks and registered at Folkestone. She was still trading in the 1920s.

The Aneroid

Brigantine   229 Tons
Built in 1874 at West Point, P.E.I.,
by Daniel C. Ramsay.
105.5′ x 25.9′ x 13.75′

Oil on canvas.
By J. Fannen, 1891.
Courtesy of the National
Maritime Museum, London, England.

The Petitcodiac River

Two of the best-known shipbuilders on the Petitcodiac River in the middle of the nineteenth century were George and Joseph Salter. In the early 1840s they had established a ship chandler's business in Saint John and soon became important shipowners. One of their first vessels was the *Jessie Amelia*, a brig of 154 tons built in 1843 by Thomas and John Bradshaw at St. Martins. In 1846 the *Tamarack*, a ship of 802 tons, was built for them by Stephen Binney at Moncton. Later that year, the Salters moved their business to Moncton and took over the Binney yard which they operated until 1857. Their first vessel was the *Hants*, a ship of 652 tons launched in 1847.

During the next ten years, with Duncan Robertson as their master builder, the Salters built more than twenty-five vessels. Many of these were large ships intended for immediate sale in England. Most of them were registered at Saint John but a few were sent over on a Governor's Pass. Three of their ships were built for Nathan DeMill of Saint John. The largest of these three was the *War Spirit*, a ship of 1317 tons built in 1854.

Apart from a few schooners, all their vessels were ships, ranging in size from 500 to 1300 tons. Their largest was the *Lady Clarendon*, a ship of 1346 tons built in 1856. Several of the Salter ships were built by Malcolm Cochran and William Spur Harris, two other Moncton shipbuilders. Many of Harris's vessels were built for Edmund Kaye, the Saint John agent for Messrs. David Cannon Son and Company of Liverpool, England. Cochran also built vessels for Kaye as well as other Saint John owners.

Shipbuilding continued in Moncton after the Salter financial failure in 1857 but on a much smaller scale. A number of large vessels were built in the 1860s by Alexander McKay and John Fisher. The largest vessel of this period was the *Excelsior*, a ship of 1231 tons built in 1864 for Nathan DeMill. Moncton became a port of registry in 1878. The last barque built in the city was the *A. E. Killam* of 1032 tons built in 1882 by Henry V. Crandall.

Apart from Hillsborough and Hopewell on the Petitcodiac River, a number of vessels were built at Alma, at the mouth of the river. The principal builder was Nathaniel H. Foster, who employed Philip C. Copeland as his foreman. In 1874 Copeland launched the *Rusiris*, a large schooner of 248 tons. Initially fitted with tow masts, she was converted into a tern schooner in 1884. The largest vessel built in the Foster yard was the *Capenhurst*, a barque of 606 tons launched in 1878.

The *Blanco*, a brigantine of 355 tons, was launched by Foster and Copeland on April 26, 1875. She was built for James Kirk and other traders of Portland, New Brunswick, who operated her for fifteen years. In January, 1891, she was dismasted and the master, Captain Tucker, having no funds to rig and fit her out, sold the vessel at Santos, Brazil.

This watercolour shows the *Blanco* under full sail. She carries four staysails and four jibs.

The Blanco

Brigantine   355 Tons
Built in 1875 at Alma, N.B.,
by N. H. Foster.
122.2' x 29.5' x 12.8'

Watercolour.
By [Edward J. Russell], undated.
Courtesy of the New Brunswick
Museum, Saint John, N.B.

William Richards

William Richards was born in 1819 at Swansea, Wales, and went to sea at the age of 18. In 1844 he was master of the *John Hawkes* of Bideford, England. This vessel was a brig of 173 tons built at St. Peters, Prince Edward Island, in 1842 by Peter Kelly. Richards made a number of voyages to the Island after 1845 in the *John Hawkes* and four years later married James Yeo's daughter, Susannah.

In 1851 Richards became one of Yeo's captains and later began to have vessels built for himself on the Island. A few of these he owned in partnership with James Yeo and he commanded a number of them himself. Gradually he began to operate independently and in 1864 established his yard at Bideford. Many of his vessels were sold in England with his brother Thomas, a ship broker in Swansea, acting as agent. From 1864 until 1892 William Richards built over ninety vessels, nearly half of which were constructed in his own yard at Bideford. The largest of these was the *Flora*, a barque of 1044 tons, launched in 1877. She remained in the Richards fleet until abandoned at sea on October 27, 1895.

The *Victoria*, a barque of 748 tons, was built by William Richards at Bideford in 1874. She was the second-largest vessel built on the Island in that year. The vessel was registered at Charlottetown and owned by the builder until 1889 when she was sold to Richard Power and Company of Swansea. A year later she passed to Norwegian ownership and was still afloat in 1904.

The *Victoria* is shown here under full sail. Her signal letters, N.M.H.F., have been hoisted at the mizzen truck and she wears the Richard Power & Company house flag at the mizzen.

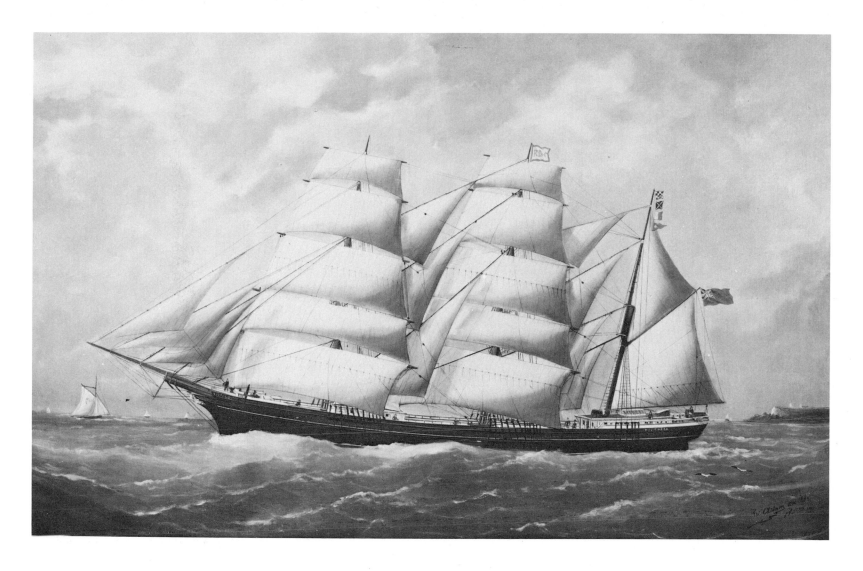

The Victoria

Barque   748 Tons
Built in 1874 at Bideford, P.E.I.,
by William Richards.
169.9′ x 34.6′ x 19.35′

Oil on canvas.
By Edward Adam, 1889.
Courtesy of the National
Maritime Museum, London, England.

The Queen of the Fleet

Barque   941 Tons
Built in 1876 at Dorchester, N.B.,
by Gideon Palmer.
171.6′ x 36.1′ x 21.0′

Oil on canvas.
By W. H. York, 1892.
Courtesy of the New Brunswick
Museum, Saint John, N.B.

The Queen of the Fleet

Shipbuilding had begun in Dorchester as early as 1825, and possibly before. By the end of the century well over one hundred vessels were built in the area. Three men dominated the shipbuilding community: Gideon Palmer and William Hickman in Dorchester and Robert Chapman, whose yard was situated across the Memramcook River at Rockland.

Gideon Palmer began building in 1854 with the construction of the *Bloomer*, a brigantine of 110 tons, and continued for the next twenty-two years, building on the average one vessel each year. Palmer owned and operated most of the vessels he built and also owned shares in a number of vessels built by Robert Chapman. All of the vessels were registered at Saint John until 1874 when Dorchester became a port of registry. When Gideon Palmer died, on June 19, 1880, the management of the yard and of the vessels was taken over by his three sons, Hiram, Barlow and Philip who built five more vessels and a small yacht.

On May 24, 1876, Gideon Palmer launched his largest and last vessel, the *Queen of the Fleet*, a barque of 941 tons. A note in the *Borderer*, on June 8, 1876, reads:

> . . . She is a fine stuanch Barque of about 1040 tons register and is in every way considered worthy of the well-known reputation of the builder. She is now lying in "Palmer's Creek" receiving spars and rigging and has been chartered by Josiah Wood and others to carry deals to Great Britain.

On June 20, 1887, the *Queen of the Fleet* sailed ". . . from Boston with a cargo of lumber bound for Buenos Ayres."[13] Her master was George Swain.

> June 24 P.M.   Fog lifted a little kept ship away S.E. by E   A.M. Fog very dense and heavy southerly swell. At 4 A.M. the ship suddenly struck on a reef and pounded heavily the tide running to the N.W. at the rate of 6 miles pr hour. The deck cargo lashings were immediately cut away and a portion of the deck cargo was thrown overboard from the starboard side in order to lighten the vessel and give her a list to port, which caused the port side of the vessel to grind upon the rocks and strain heavily on the bilge. Launched two boats with stern anchors & 4½ in. hawser, to be in readiness if required, to warp the ship off; but in a short space of time, on account of the heavy surf, the boats were partly filled and stove, and the anchors and hawsers were totally lost in getting the boats on board the ship. Set fore and upper topsails, topgallant sails, flying jib, mizzen topmast stay sail, all the sails the ship could bear in order if possible to press her off the reef. 7.30 A.M. the tide began to rise: the wind increasing to a gale from S.S.W. and with the assistance of the sails, the ship commenced to move and gradually worked off the reef.[14]

The vessel put into Halifax where she arrived on July 1. She was put on the Marine Railway at Dartmouth and the necessary repairs were carried out. She remained in the Palmer fleet for another eight years. On May 24, 1895, the vessel was sold at Liverpool, England, for £600 to Swedish subjects and later renamed the *Rhea*. In 1907, as the *Uniao*, she was under Portuguese ownership.

The *Queen of the Fleet* is shown in this painting close-hauled on the port tack. She is entering harbour and signaling for a pilot. Her signal letters, Q.F.G.K., are hoisted at the mizzen truck.

The Colchester

James E. Dickie began as a general merchant in Upper Stewiacke in 1856 and, like many "landsmen", purchased shares in vessels which were operated by other men. In this case the managing owner was his brother, John B. Dickie, a banker in Truro.

Between 1872 and 1891 James Dickie's records[15] indicate that he owned shares in three barques and three ships, all belonging to the Dickie fleet. One of these was the *Colchester*, a ship of 1384 tons built at Princeport, Nova Scotia, by John Sanderson in 1875 and registered at Halifax. The contract price, calculated at $28 per ton on 1634 tons carpenter's measure, amounted to $45,752. However, there were financial difficulties, and an additional $6,400 was required before the vessel was outfitted and ready for sea.

The letters of John to his brother give detailed information on the voyages, cargoes and profits of all their vessels. Unlike many ship owners, whose letters are filled with rantings and ravings against agents and captains, John's letters are very mild, and at times even philosophical. This splendid letter gives information on the *Linden*, a barque of 913 tons built at Clifton, Nova Scotia, by James Crowe and launched a few months earlier.

Truro, Dec. 13, 1881

Dear Bro.

In reply to your enquiries about the LINDEN: I went to Saint John myself and investigated the matter. The Capt took his father from home for pilot. The old man had been acquainted with the coast in earlier life, but things didn't look along the shore as they used to, and the result was he got her ashore where she had no business to be. Even then, when warned by a St. John pilot that they were in great danger, they rejected his offered services thinking they could get out of it without but instead of that it came on a heavy blow drove the ship on the reef of rocks where she pounded for three hours and finally dragging over into deep water, was saved from utter destruction, by a tug being got from St. John and taking her into the harbour — being kept afloat by steady pumping, but was full of water when she reached the blocks. Under almost any ordinary circumstances she must have been a total wreck. But Kind Providence spared us from that this time. It was a serious blunder however on the part of the captain — and will likely be a good lesson to him in future.

. . . .

The cost of repairs were estimated by the inspector when I was there at seven or eight thousand dollars — and may be more. . . .

The "Colchester" had to put back to land again after being out to sea 12 days — consequently we miss chartering her *"to arrive"* which was about effected at a pretty good rate. The "Bedford" came into Halifax for repairs lately. It has been a fearful time this fall — still, so far as known, the vessels are all in existence yet, but they are not making much money at present. We should be thankful they are not lost, as so many have been. Shipowning has its cares and troubles as well as other things.[16]

The *Colchester* remained in the Dickie fleet until 1893 when she was sold to Norwegians and renamed *Bellevue*. She was still afloat in 1907.

The vessel is shown in this painting entering harbour under full sail. The signal for a pilot has been hoisted at the fore truck and the ship's signal letters, P.F.T.Q., at the monkey gaff. The Dickie house flag is being worn at the mainmast.

The Colchester

Ship   1384 Tons
Built in 1875 at Princeport, N.S.,
by John Sanderson.
216.0′ x 40.0′ x 23.75′

Oil on canvas.
Unsigned and undated.
Courtesy of the Nova Scotia
Museum, Halifax, N.S.

Crank Windlass.

Wooden Windlass, with Improved Purchase.

By the middle of the nineteenth century great improvements had been made in methods of navigation. Nautical charts of most parts of the world were readily available and there were many books on navigation, tide tables and sailing directions for most ports.

This photograph shows some of the instruments, books and charts in common use in the late 1870s. They are, from left to right:

T. Walker's patent log — an instrument towed behind a vessel, the dials indicating the distance travelled over a period of time. From this information the speed of the vessel could be calculated.

A book, *Sailing Directions for the Navigation Round Ireland*, published by James Imray & Son, London, 1873.

A sextant — used for measuring horizontal and vertical angles in navigation.

A copy of *The American Coast Pilot* by Edmund M. Blunt, first published in 1863. The book contains "directions for Principal Harbours, Capes and Headlands, on the coast of North and Part of South America, describing the Soundings, Bearings of the Lighthouses and Beacons from the Rocks, Shoals, Ledges, &c and the Latitudes and Longitudes of the Principal Harbours and Capes together with Tide Tables and Variation."

A telescope and a ship's log book.

The instruments and books are placed on *An Outline Chart of the World*, 1872. In the foreground is a set of dividers used for taking a course, or bearing, from the compass on the chart.

From the J. Snelling & Co.
Catalogue of Ship, Steamboat and Yacht Fixtures,
New York, 1874.

Courtesy of the Dalhousie
University Archives, Halifax, N.S.

Charts, books and nautical instruments

David Lynch

When she was launched on July 22, 1876, the *Alexander Yeats*, a ship of 1589 tons, was said to be the finest ship ever built in the Saint John area.[17] While this remark has undoubtedly been made about many vessels, David Lynch, her builder, held a very high reputation as a designer and shipbuilder.

Born in Ireland in 1835, David Lynch came to Saint John with his parents when he was a young lad of nine. He apprenticed in the shipyard of George King and in 1861 he built his first vessel, the *Richard Simonds*, a schooner of 45 tons.

In 1875 Lynch launched his largest vessel, the *Rock Terrace*, a ship of 1768 tons. Built for the Troop fleet, she was one of the largest ships constructed in Saint John since the time of the Wrights. In March, 1888, the vessel was abandoned at sea off Guam and drifted without a crew for five months before finally going ashore on Tarawa Island.

From 1877 until 1884 Lynch built eight more vessels for the Troop fleet and one for Robert Thomson. In 1894 he built what was probably his best-known vessel, the *David Lynch*, a small pilot schooner of 65 tons. She remained in service in Saint John for many years. His last two vessels were steamers: the *Lord Kitchener*, of 109 tons built in 1903, and the *Senlac* of 687 tons built in 1904. He died in September 1904.

The *Alexander Yeats*, named after her owner, remained in the Yeats fleet for eighteen years. On September 20, 1894, the vessel was sold to George Windram and registered at Liverpool, England. In September, 1896, she was driven ashore on the Cornish coast, near Penzance, England.

The *Alexander Yeats* is shown here, aground near Penzance in 1896. The photograph gives some indication of the condition in which the sails and running rigging were left after the vessel struck.

Ship   1589 Tons
Built in 1876 at Portland, N.B.,
by David Lynch.
218.2′ x 40.2′ x 24.0′

The Alexander Yeats

Courtesy of the Nova Scotia
Museum, Halifax, N.S.
Frederick William Wallace
Collection.

Hantsport, Nova Scotia

The two leading shipbuilders and shipowners in Hantsport, Nova Scotia, were Ezra Churchill and John B. North. Between them they dominated shipbuilding activity for more than seventy-five years. Churchill was born in 1804. His name first appeared in the Shelburne Shipping Register in 1820 when he was master and owner of the *Catherine*, a schooner of 24 tons, and one of the many American vessels captured during the War of 1812.

Churchill gradually increased the number of vessels that he owned and after the 1850s was having vessels built at Hantsport by Jacob Lockhart, Daniel Huntley, Elisha E. Fuller and John Davison. Apart from operating his own fleet, Churchill owned shares in vessels built by Jonathan E. Steel for Sheffield and Wickwire, and in vessels built and owned by Shubael Dimock of Windsor. When Ezra Churchill died, in 1874, the business was taken over by his sons George W. and John, who continued building and operating the Churchill fleet until the early part of the twentieth century.

John B. North began shipbuilding in 1852 with the construction of the *Clyde*, a small brigantine of 126 tons. Over the next forty-two years he built more than fifty vessels. In 1864 he launched his first large vessel, the *Guiona*, a barque of 654 tons, and in 1877 his first ship, the *Forest King* of 1602 tons. North built three more ships: the *Wallace* of 1583 tons in 1882, the *Landsdown* of 1486 tons in 1884, and the *Loodiana* of 1874 tons, his largest vessel, in 1889. This is the ship mentioned in the diary[18] of Alice Coalfleet. The *Loodiana* was burnt at sea on January 16, 1891, with the loss of all hands.

In 1887 Gideon Bigelow designed and began building a brigantine in the Bigelow shipyard at Canning. The keel was laid and the vessel partly in frames when the parties who had ordered the vessel withdrew. The partly completed hull was purchased by North but, rather than finish the vessel in the Bigelow yard, he had the frames dismantled and transported to Hantsport, and the vessel was completed in North's yard. When launched she was named the *G. B. Lockhart*.

As the demand for barques and ships dropped, North switched to building barquentines and in 1892 built two four-masted schooners, the *Gypsum Prince* and the *Gypsum Empress*, both of 723 tons, for the Gypsum Packet Company of Windsor. John B. North's last vessel was the *Curacao*, a brigantine of 284 tons, built in 1894. Ten years later his son, David Ellis North, built the *Clemencia*, a schooner of 123 tons. She was the last of the North vessels.

This painting shows the *Forest King* with all sails set except the cross-jack which has been clewed up to the yard. The vessel carries double topsails but single topgallants. A fore topsail studdingsail has been set on the port side. An unusual feature is the loose-footed gaff mainsail.

The *Forest King* remained in the North fleet for twenty-two years. In July, 1899, she was sold to Italian subjects, renamed *Marina Madre* and registered at Genoa, Italy. The vessel was converted into a hulk in 1913.

The Forest King

Ship   1602 Tons
Built in 1877 at Hantsport, N.S.,
by John B. North.
213.6′ x 41.0′ x 24.4′

Oil on canvas.
Unsigned and undated.
Courtesy of the Public Archives
of Nova Scotia, Halifax, N.S.

Beaconsfield

"Beaconsfield" represents one of the many fine Victorian mansions built and owned by shipbuilders and shipowners throughout the Maritime provinces. The house was built in 1877 by James Peak, a prominent shipping merchant of Charlottetown, Prince Edward Island. It was later purchased by Henry James Cundall, and on his death, in 1916, it was turned into a girls' residence. The building was acquired by the Prince Edward Island Heritage Foundation in 1972 and has now been restored.

The Great Fire

Lithograph.
Drawn by E. J. Russell.

Courtesy of Mr. Charles De Volpi,
St-Sauveur-des-Monts, Quebec.

On June 20, 1877, a disastrous fire swept through Saint John, New Brunswick. Almost all of the city south of King Street was completely destroyed. This included the entire business section. The loss to shipping, however, was slight. Most vessels in the harbour floated down to places of safety, although a number of woodboats at the head of the market slip and a number of schooners moored at the end of the wharves were burnt. This view was sketched by Edward J. Russell, from Carleton, during the height of the fire.

The Barquentine

In 1838, Dennis Horton built the *Loyalist*, a vessel of 186 tons, at Yarmouth, Nova Scotia. When she was registered at Halifax in the fall of that year, she was described as a three-masted brigantine. However, when reregistered at Yarmouth in 1840 the vessel was described as a barque. Fourteen years later, in 1852, the *Vivid* of 91 tons was built by Charles MacLeod at Liverpool. She was also described as a three-masted brigantine but when reregistered at Saint John, New Brunswick, in 1853, she appeared as a three-masted schooner. While it is impossible to say definitely without contemporary plans or descriptions, these two vessels may have been the first two barquentines built in the Maritimes.

In 1853, the *Reserve*, a barquentine of 452 tons, was built at Tatamagouche by Campbell and Millar, and registered at Pictou. This is the first appearance of the term barquentine in a shipping register in the Maritime Provinces.

Since the barquentine carried square sails on the foremast, she could carry a large sail area when running before the wind. However, the vessel was more lightly sparred than a barque, was easier to handle and required a smaller crew.

A few barquentines were built in the late 1850s and 1860s but it was not until after 1870 that the rig became popular. Toward the end of the nineteenth century a number of four-masted barquentines were built. One of these was the *Ensenada* of 1072 tons, built at South Maitland in 1889 by W. P. Cameron.

The first barquentine constructed in Prince Edward Island was the *Zeta* of 164 tons, built at Vernon River in 1868 and owned by Lemuel Cambridge Owen. After 1872 several builders and owners, including James Duncan, William Richards, John Yeo and James Peak, tried out the new rig; ten barquentines were built in 1875 and nine in 1876.

On May 3, 1877 John McDougall launched the *Vigilant*, a barquentine of 399 tons at Dundas for Lemuel Cambridge Owen and William Welsh. On September 13, 1878, William Welsh became sole owner and the vessel was reported missing a month later.

This spar plan of the *Vigilant* shows clearly the standing rigging of a barquentine and the position of the masts, yards and the fore and aft sails. The fore upper topsail, topgallant and royal yards are shown in the lowered position. As can be seen from the dimensions, the main and mizzen masts are the same length.

Vigilant
DIMENSIONS OF SPARS
(in feet)

Spar	Fore	Main	Mizzen
Mast — deck to truck	104	110	110
Lower mast — deck to cap	44	65	65
Topmast	38	56	56
Topgallant and royal mast	39		
Lower yard	64		
Lower topmast yard	56		
Upper topmast yard	54		
Topgallant yard	44		
Royal yard	34		
Boom		30	42
Gaff		28	28
Jib-boom	43		

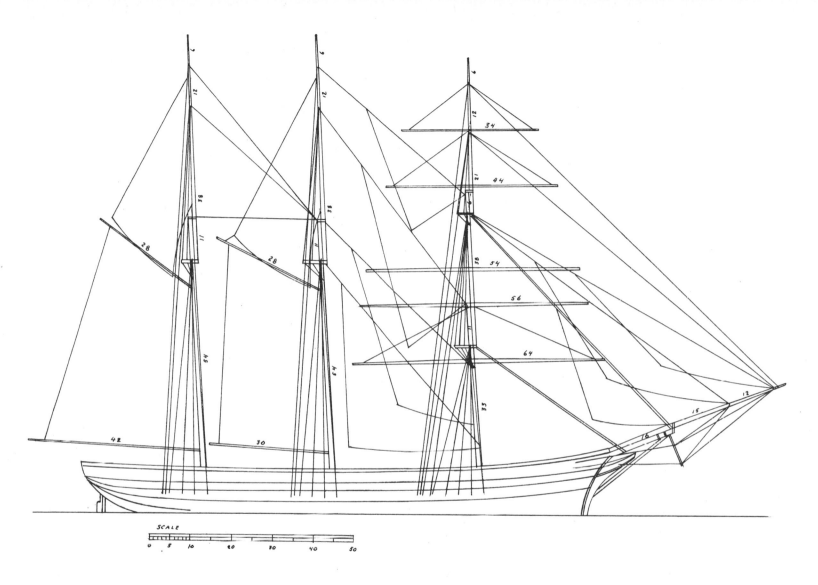

The Vigilant

Barquentine   399 Tons
Built in 1877 at Dundas, P.E.I.,
by John McDougall.
131.3′ x 29.0′ x 14.95′

Spar plan: courtesy of the Prince
Edward Island Heritage Foundation,
Charlottetown, P.E.I.
Traced by Charles A. Armour.

The crew of the Agnes Sutherland

Ship   1134 Tons
Built in 1875 at St. Martins, N.B.,
by William H. Rourke.
193.1' x 36.0' x 22.0'

Courtesy of the Nova Scotia
Museum, Halifax, N.S.
Frederick William Wallace
Collection.

The Agnes Sutherland

While the crews of many small coastal vessels were often local men who were known and trusted by the master and owners, this was not the case in the large ocean-going vessels. The master, who was often part owner, was frequently from the home port. The crew, however, were from many different countries and ranged in age from sixteen to fifty. Often they were rough men, and fights, semimutinies and desertions were very common.

This photograph shows the crew of the *Agnes Sutherland* in San Francisco Bay in 1880. The men are standing in front of the mainmast. The third man from the right is the mate. The coaming of the main hatch can be seen in the foreground.

The *Agnes Sutherland* was registered at Saint John and owned by Amasa Durkee, a merchant of Liverpool, England. The vessel was sold in 1885 and registered at London, England, until 1887 when she was sold to the Norwegians and renamed *Prince Victor*. She was still afloat in 1905.

The Arklow

This photograph of the *Arklow*, taken from the roof of the after-cabin on the quarter-deck, looking forward, shows very clearly details of the deck, masts, yards and rigging. The mizzen spanker runs on a separate mast abaft the mizzenmast. The small figure, forward, is standing on the forecastle deck.

The *Arklow* was owned by Nicholas Mosher, Frederick Curry and other merchants of Windsor and Newport. The vessel was wrecked on the west side of Bute Island, Scotland, on December 20, 1894.

Ship   1474 Tons
Built in 1879 at Avondale, N.S.,
by Nicholas Mosher.
214.0′ x 40.0′ x 24.0′

Courtesy of the Nova Scotia
Museum, Halifax, N.S.

The Plymouth

It was not uncommon for the wife of a captain to go to sea with her husband, and their children often accompanied them. George Coalfleet was master of the barque *Plymouth* from 1886 to 1892, and for most of this period his wife Alice* travelled with him. Her diary,[19] kept during this time, gives a warm picture of life on board a sailing ship from a woman's point of view. A few extracts are quoted here.

August 18th, 1886.   We anchored in Royal Roads. Go ashore to Victoria a very quaint little town nestled among the trees. Dodd and I like this little very English spot and we think it would be a good plan to settle when we give up going to sea.

. . . .

Saturday, December 25th, 1886.   A merry Christmas in the Yellow Sea. We have chicken and mince pie for dinner. We wonder about the folks at home and wish them a happy day. We are having head winds which does not add to the holiday spirit.
Saturday, January 1st, 1887.   New Year's Day — I wish all my friends and enemies (if I have any) a very Happy New Year. We are rejoicing over a fair wind and have made Shantung Promontory and pass the lighthouse.

. . . .

Monday, July 18th, 1887.   Long. 139–19 Latitude 36.59. Dodd and I sat up in the Pilot House. He was making bullets for his gun and I looked on. I retired at 7:30 trying to read but other matters require my attention. At 10 o'clock a little stranger makes his appearance. he is very welcome. a dear pretty little fellow his little head covered with black hair — Dodd is doctor nurse and everything else, washes and dresses the little one, then stands and recites funny poetry to make me forget my pain.

In February, 1889, while at Plymouth, England, she saw her sister Lucy whom she had not seen for five years. A month later she left the *Plymouth* at Bristol, England, to return to Hantsport. A second son, George, was born on June 18, and she rejoined her husband in New York on September 28 with the two children.

* Alice Coalfleet (nee Allen) was a niece of, and her husband George was a a first cousin of, Hiram and Abel Coalfleet.

In March, 1890, while at Montevideo, she had an opportunity to see her brother Woodbury, who was on the *Loanda*.

Saturday, Dec. 20th, 1890 [Shanghai]   Receive our letters, one containing sad news for me poor old Woody dies on the passage from Montevedeo to New York of fever and was buried at sea so glad I saw the dear boy in Montevedeo. Just we three girls left. Lucy, Rena and me.

. . . .

Sunday, June 14th, 1891 [New York]   We are planning to leave the PLYMOUTH. go to Hantsport and in the Spring go out to British Columbia.

Alice and Dodd left the *Plymouth* on June 18 and returned to Hantsport.

Tuesday, Sept. 8th, 1891.   Receive sad news from London — poor Lucy died in childbirth. I cable Father. Well only Rena and I left now.

Rena's husband Miles Boyd was the master of the *Loodiana* and when the vessel arrived in New York on November 2, Alice wired her sister to come to Hantsport.

Wednesday, Nov. 18th.   Rena arrives on the 6 o'clock train. Such a joy for we had not seen each other since we were married — we talked and yearned for Lucy and Woody.

. . . .

Saturday, Nov. 21st.   George Churchill wants Dodd to go to New York and take the "Hamburg" for one trip to London so he thinks he better go.

Dodd joined the *Hamburg* in New York and sailed for England on December 1. Alice accompanied her sister back to New York.

. . . .

Monday, December 14th.   I leave for Hantsport. Rena hates for me to leave even tried to get me to go with them and join in London — but I just could not leave the babies — and so we say goodbye.
Monday, December 28th, 1891.   The "Hamburg" arrives in London today 24 day passage. Hope the "Loodiana" will soon arrive too.

The Plymouth

Barque   1312 Tons
Built in 1879 at Hantsport, N.S.,
by John Davison.
198.0' x 40.0' x 23.3'

Oil on canvas.
By J. O'Brien, 1881.
Courtesy of the Public Archives
of Nova Scotia, Halifax, N.S.

Wednesday, Feb. 17th. Go to Windsor to see what I can find out about the "Loodiana" a burning ship was sighted off Land's End, which seems to be the "Loodiana" I am sick over it. Rena's birthday soon 23 so young to die.

. . . .

Wednesday, April 6th. The "Loodiana" was burnt at sea on January 16th off Land's End — sighted by two british steamers. The S.S. "British Monarch" went to aid them but the ship was aflame. The newspaper accounts (New York papers) gave heart-rending accounts of the disaster. She was loaded with Naptha. I am just heart weary — and now we are beginning to get anxious about the "Hamburg". In less than two years I have lost my only brother and two sisters and now I am the only one left. I wonder how Father feels about it all.

Monday, April 11th, 1892. A telegram this morning — the Hamburg's arrival in New York and the saddest news of all — for Dodd died at sea on Feb. 28th — I had a premonition that something was wrong but cast it aside as foolish anxiety — but it is all too true. May my little boys be spared me — they do not realise their loss.

The *Plymouth* was owned by George W. and John Churchill until 1898. The vessel passed through several owners and was converted into a barge in 1908. The painting of the *Plymouth* was done by John O'Brien, a Halifax artist. The vessel is shown under reduced canvas entering harbour and signaling for a pilot. She wears the Churchill house flag at the main truck and the Red Ensign at the spanker gaff. Her signal letters, T.D.C.F., have been hoisted at the mizzen truck.

The Kate F. Troop

The 1860s saw the establishment of a number of major shipyards at Black River, Gardners Creek, and Tynemouth Creek in Saint John County, New Brunswick.

John McLeod began building at Black River in 1862 with the construction of the *Brilliant*, a brig of 262 tons. Later he was joined by his brother Robert. Between 1871 and 1878 many of their vessels were built for Luke Stewart of Saint John. In later years they built for the Troop fleet and also operated some of their own vessels.

In 1878 they built the *New City*, a ship of 1441 tons, named to commemorate the rebuilding of Saint John after the fire of 1877. Their largest vessel was the *John McLeod*, a ship of 1595 tons built in 1885 and their last, the *Malwa*, a barquentine of 539 tons, was launched in 1901.

In 1862 William Wallace, in partnership with Robert Lovett, built his first vessel, the *Fredonia*, a schooner of 88 tons, at Tynemouth Creek. Four years later he began building larger vessels and, in partnership with his brothers Robert and John, continued until 1899. Their largest vessel was the *Hospodar*, a ship of 1549 tons, launched in 1874 for George T. Soley of Liverpool, England.

When his partnership with Richard Lovett dissolved shortly after 1854, John Stewart Parker continued to build at Tynemouth Creek. From 1858 until 1883 he built almost entirely for the Troop fleet. His largest vessel was the *Empress of India*, a ship of 1713 tons, launched in 1874.

The *Kate F. Troop*, a barque of 1097 tons, was built by Parker in 1881. The vessel remained in the Troop fleet until 1907 and two years later was transferred to Argentinian ownership.

This weather view of the *Kate F. Troop* shows fine rigging detail. The vessel wears the Troop house flag at the main and the barque's signal letters, T.B.H.J., have been hoisted at the mizzen truck.

The Kate F. Troop

Barque   1097 Tons
Built in 1881 at Tynemouth Creek, N.B.,
by John S. Parker.
187.0′ x 37.5′ x 22.1′

Oil on canvas.
Unsigned and undated.
Courtesy of Mr. & Mrs. Douglas
Brown, St. Martins, N.B.

Taylor Brothers, Saint John

John Fletcher Taylor in partnership with his brother Charles Edward Taylor and John Peabody Burpee operated under the name of Taylor Brothers in Saint John. From 1870 until 1904 they owned and operated a fleet of seventeen vessels and also owned shares in four more vessels owned by other men.[20] Most of these were large barques and ships from 900 to 1400 tons and all but one were built especially for the company.

Their first vessel was the *Stella*, a large brigantine of 445 tons built at Port Elgin in 1870 by E. H. Ogden. Another, the *Assyria*, a barque of 724 tons, was built at Sackville by George Anderson in 1872. From 1871 until 1878 Robert Chapman built six vessels for Taylor Brothers at his yard at Rockland and the company in turn owned shares in two more of Chapman's vessels. From 1879 until 1887 all of their vessels were built by Oliver Pittfield, the shipbuilder from Saint John who had supervised the construction of the *Robert Godfrey* in 1868.

Oliver Pittfield had worked in partnership with James F. Cruikshanks from 1872 until 1877 and built eight large vessels, five of which were over 1400 tons. Most of these were built for Zebedee Ring of Saint John. The largest of these was the *General Domville*, a ship of 1569 tons launched in 1876.

After 1877 Oliver Pittfield built eight ships and barques for Taylor Brothers. The largest of these and the largest in the Taylor Brothers fleet was the *Albania*, a ship of 1438 tons built in 1884. In 1890 he launched the *Vaneen*, a barquentine of 542 tons for George G. Lovitt of Yarmouth. While Pittfield was primarily a builder, he often owned shares in the vessels he built.

The *Africa*, a barque of 1146 tons, was built by Oliver Pittfield in 1879 and launched on May 22. When she was registered at Saint John on June 10 her owners were John and Charles Taylor, John P. C. Burpee, Francis Collins, Edwin J. Everett, Oliver Pittfield and David Murray, the master. The vessel remained under the Taylor house flag for thirteen years and traded regularly across the Atlantic. On June 8, 1892, she was abandoned at sea in Lat. 40° 12′ S., Long. 35° 3′W. The crew were saved.

This painting of the *Africa* gives especially fine detail and shows the vessel close-hauled on the starboard tack. The barque's signal letters, S.W.H.D., have been hoisted at the mizzen truck.

The Africa

Barque   1146 Tons
Built in 1879 at Saint John, N.B.,
by Oliver Pittfield.
183.5' x 36.4' x 22.3'

Oil on canvas.
Unsigned and undated.
Courtesy of Mr. Fred Taylor,
Rothesay, N.B.

Newcastle, N.B. Vessels loading timber at Ritchies' Wharf

Courtesy of the Provincial Archives of New Brunswick, Fredericton, N.B.

The vessel at the wharf is the *Norman*, a barque of 870 tons built at Maitland, Nova Scotia, in 1877 by Alexander MacDougall. The vessel docking is the *G. S. Penry*, a barque of 737 tons built at Black River, New Brunswick, in 1876 by John and Robert McLeod. The photograph was probably taken in the 1890s when the *Norman* was registered at Liverpool, England.

Nova Scotia Shipmasters

Courtesy of the Nova Scotia Museum, Halifax, N.S. Frederick William Wallace Collection.

This photograph was taken in Newcastle, New South Wales, Australia, to commemorate the chance meeting there of five Nova Scotia captains. Standing, from left to right, are: Varne Doty of Yarmouth and O. H. Henderson of Halifax. Seated, from left to right, are: Everett MacDougall of Maitland, Henry Nickerson of Shelburne and Captain Crosby of Yarmouth.

The E. J. Spicer

Advocate, Spencer's Island, Parrsboro, Five Islands, Economy, Londonderry, and the Minas Basin shore had been a scene of active shipbuilding since the early nineteenth century. Parrsboro was created a port of registry in 1850. Most of the vessels were small schooners, brigs and brigantines and nearly all were locally owned.

One of the most famous of these vessels was the *Amazon,* a brigantine of 198 tons built by Joshua Dewis in 1860 and registered at Parrsboro in 1861. While the shipping register gives the port of construction as Parrsboro, it is believed that the *Amazon* was one of the first vessels built at Spencer's Island.

In 1867 the *Amazon* was wrecked at "Big Glace Bay,"[21] Cape Breton, then salvaged, sold and later registered at Sydney. In 1868 she was transferred to American ownership, registered at New York and renamed *Mary Celeste.* In 1872 this vessel was found drifting off the Azores, deserted by her crew.

Not only has there been wild speculation as to what happened to the *Mary Celeste,* but the actual events have been embellished and distorted. The evidence is best summarized in the book by Charles Edey Fay in which he gives a possible explanation of what may have happened. The exact fate of the crew of the *Mary Celeste* will never be known.

One of the largest vessels constructed in the area was the *E. J. Spicer,* a ship of 1317 tons built at Spencer's Island in 1880 by Amasa Loomer. She was owned by the master, George D. Spicer, and a number of other men from the area. This vessel is best known for an incident which occurred on August 4, 1882 while the vessel was lying at anchor in New York Harbour. The mate, Daniel Spicer, went forward to the forecastle and ordered Patrick Creay, one of the crew who had just come on board, to fetch a tackle. When the seaman made a rude reply, the mate is reported to have kicked him. Losing his temper, Creay armed himself with a capstan bar and a fight ensued. When Spicer eventually managed to get the bar from him, Creay drew a knife and stabbed him in the side. Spicer died almost immediately.

In court, the evidence was contradictory. One of the crew claimed that Creay had attacked the mate. Creay, on the other hand, pleaded self-defence and got off with a fairly light sentence.

For deep-sea vessels, the problem of getting reliable crews was a very serious one. While there were many able men who knew their trade and behaved well, there were others who were completely incompetent. Many were supplied by the "crimps" who made money by rounding up men and supplying crews to the masters. A large proportion of these men had little or no knowledge of the sea and many were fugitives from justice. Often they arrived on board drunk.

With such a mixed lot of men, fights were common and the traditional belaying pin often served as a convenient weapon. The fault was not always on the side of the seamen, however; and there are many stories of brutality by mates and captains. In many cases knives were drawn; often there were serious injuries and occasionally, as in the case of the *E. J. Spicer,* death was the result.

The *E. J. Spicer* remained on the Parrsboro register until she passed to Norwegian ownership in 1905.

This splendid painting of the *E. J. Spicer* was done by A. Jacobsen, a well-known American marine artist of Hoboken, New Jersey. The vessel is under reduced canvas; the royals and topgallants have been furled. The deck and rigging detail is especially fine. The Canadian Red Ensign is being worn at the spanker gaff.

The E. J. Spicer

Ship   1317 Tons
Built in 1880 at Spencer's Island, N.S.,
by Amasa Loomer.
203.5' x 39.7' x 23.8'

Oil on canvas.
By A. Jacobsen, 1881.
Courtesy of Mr. John Bigelow,
Halifax, N.S.

The Elsie

The years after 1877 saw a rapid decline in shipbuilding in Prince Edward Island. Although a few barques and barquentines were built, most of the vessels were small schooners and nearly all were locally owned. Apart from the general decrease in the demand for wooden sailing ships, the great timber supplies were rapidly being exhausted. The last large vessels built on the Island were both launched in 1884: the *Charles E. Lefurgey*, a barque of 950 tons built by J. Lefurgey at Summerside and the *Auriga*, a barque of 887 tons built by William Richards at Bideford. Both vessels were owned by their builders.

In 1881 only fifteen new vessels were built. The largest of these was the *Parthenia*, a barque of 749 tons built by William Richards at Bideford.

Edwin Coffin built vessels at Mount Stewart and Souris for a number of owners including Lemuel Cambridge Owen and James Peak. This spar plan came from the family of Lemuel Cambridge Owen and is marked "Brig at Coffins, 1881". It can therefore be positively identified as the *Elsie*, a brig of 316 tons built at Souris by Edwin Coffin in 1881 and launched on October 10. The vessel was registered at Charlottetown on October 29 and owned by Lemuel Cambridge Owen. Her master was Laughlin McNeill. The vessel had a very short career. Less than two years after launching, on March 4, 1883, she was lost at Matanzas, Cuba.

The plan shows clearly the brig rig. The upper topsail, topgallant and royal yards are shown in the lowered position on the foremast and in the raised position on the mainmast.

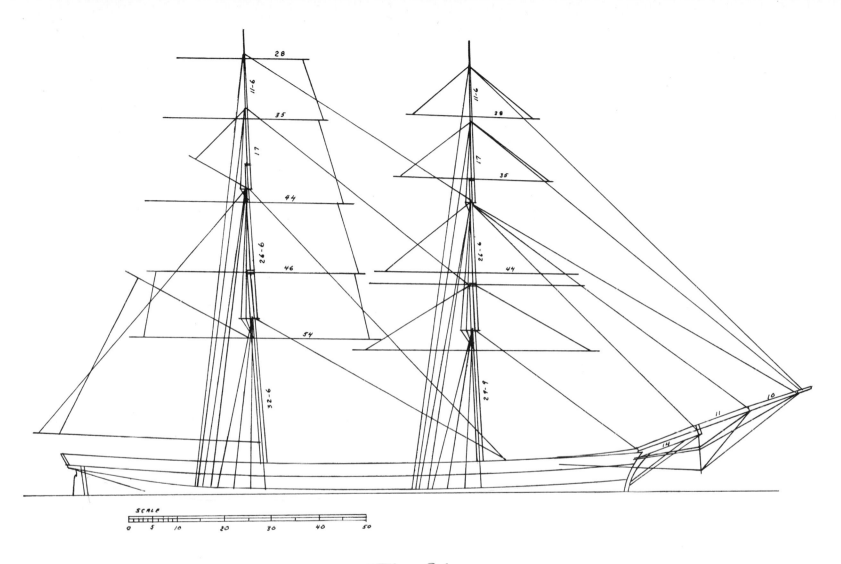

SCALE

0 5 10   20   30   40   50

The Elsie

Brig   316 Tons
Built in 1881 at Souris, P.E.I.,
by Edwin Coffin.
119.6′ x 26.8′ x 14.95′

Original spar plan: courtesy of
the Prince Edward Island Heritage
Foundation, Charlottetown, P.E.I.
Traced by Charles A. Armour.

Pictou County

The major shipbuilding centres along the Northumberland Strait shore of Nova Scotia were located at Tatamagouche, River John, Pictou, New Glasgow, Wallace and Pugwash. Pictou opened as a port of registry in 1840 and between twenty and forty new vessels were registered each year. Of the many hundreds of builders in this area only a few of the more prominent can be mentioned here.

One of the first vessels built at Tatamagouche was the *Elizabeth*, a schooner of 91 tons built by Joseph McKeel in 1824 for Alexander Campbell, George Smith and William Mortimer. For a few years Campbell built in partnership with his brothers William and James, but from 1835 until his death in 1854 he built entirely on his own. In the 1840s and 1850s he was building four or five vessels a year, mainly small schooners and brigs and a few barques of around 400 tons. After 1854 the yard was operated by Campbell's sons, David and Archie, and in 1872 they launched the largest of the Campbell vessels, the *Jumna*, a ship of 877 tons.

George MacKenzie's first vessel was the *James William*, a schooner of 42 tons built at Pictou by James Reid in 1821. For a short time after 1840 MacKenzie built at Shipyard Point, near Trenton, but he soon moved to New Glasgow. Most of his vessels were built in the yard of his brother-in-law James Carmichael, another prominent builder. By the 1850s the number and size of MacKenzie's vessels had increased. His three largest were the *Catherine Glen*, a ship of 1320 tons built in 1852; the *Hamilton Campbell Kidston*, a ship of 1444 tons built in 1851; and the *Magna Charta*, a ship of 1465 tons built in 1854.

Gradually the yard was taken over by MacKenzie's nephew James William Carmichael, who eventually operated one of the largest fleets of vessels out of New Glasgow. He was one of the few to purchase steel sailing ships and steamers from England.

Two of the best-known shipyards at River John were those of the James Kitchens (Senior and Junior) and Archibald MacKenzie. James Kitchen Sr. began in 1845 with the building of the *Express*, a brigantine of 103 tons. By 1850 he was joined by his son James Jr. The designer and foreman of the yard was Duncan Johnson. His largest vessel, and the largest built in Pictou County, was the *Warrior*, a ship of 1687 tons launched from the Kitchen yard on August 21, 1884. In the same year, Archibald MacKenzie, Kitchen's rival since 1848, built the *Caldera*, a ship of 1574 tons.

While James Kitchen was the principal shareholder in the *Warrior*, the managing owner was Alexander C. MacDonald, a merchant of Pictou. Six other local residents also held shares, as well as John Walter Scammell, a ship broker in New York. The vessel was sold to Italian interests in 1899 and was still under the Italian flag in 1907.

The *Warrior* was a three skysail yarder; she carried skysails on her fore, main and mizzen. She is shown in this painting with a full set of sails: courses, lower and upper topsails, lower and upper topgallants, royals and skysails. The ship's signal letters, W.B.Q.F., have been hoisted inferior to the Canadian Red Ensign being worn at the monkey gaff.

The Warrior

Ship   1687 Tons
Built in 1884 at River John, N.S.,
by James Kitchen.
221.0′ x 40.5′ x 24.2′

Oil on canvas.
By John Loos, 1895.
Courtesy of the Public Archives
of Nova Scotia, Halifax, N.S.

The G. A. Smith

In 1882, the Canadian Government ". . . as an aid to develop the sea fisheries, to encourage the building and fitting out of improved fishing craft as well as to ameliorate the condition of fisherman . . ."[22] authorized the payment of $150,000 per year in fishing bounties. Canadian fishing vessels of over 10 tons which were engaged in fishing for a three-month period were entitled to a bounty of $2.00 per ton up to 80 tons. One-half of the bounty went to the owners and one-half to the crew. The bounty was also extended to fishing boats and their crews.

From 1884 to 1895 the bounty varied from $3.00 to $1.00 per ton depending on the vessel's size. From 1896 until 1913 it remained at $1.00 per ton. The result was an increase in the number of fishing schooners built in the Maritime Provinces.

From 1882 until 1913 an average of 500 to 600 vessels per year in Nova Scotia, 150 to 250 vessels per year in New Brunswick and 20 to 30 vessels per year in Prince Edward Island received the bounty. One-third of all the Nova Scotia vessels were registered at Lunenburg.

One of the vessels affected by the new regulation was the *G. A. Smith*, a schooner of 95 tons built at Lunenburg in 1884 by James Maxner. The following list of owners,[23] all from Lunenburg, reveals the financial improvement of many people in the community in shipping.

		Shares
William Young	Shipping Master	8
Abraham Smith	Mariner	8
William C. Smith	Mariner	4
C. Albert Smith	Carpenter	4
James Maxner	Shipbuilder	4
Henry Dauphinee	Blockmaker	8
Joseph Dauphinee	Blockmaker	4
Charles Edward Kaulback	Gentleman	8
Charles W. H. Kaulback	Law Student	16
		64 Shares

Although shares were bought and sold at regular intervals, William Young remained managing owner. In February 1902 the schooner was sold for $1,500 to G. W. Robertson and T. O. Murray, traders of Richibucto, and the vessel was registered at that port. She was wrecked on January 5, 1907.

The sail plan of the *G. A. Smith* by Harry Ham of Lunenburg is unusual in that it shows the position of all the cloths. The vessel carries an outer jib on the fore capstay and a standing jib on the forestay. The sheet of the standing jib is attached to a short club. The schooner also carries topsails on the fore and main and a fisherman's staysail which is set flying below the main topmast stay. The location of the reef points is shown on the foresail, mainsail and standing jib. Superimposed on the mainsail is the outline of a small storm trysail for use in weather that would not permit the setting of a double-reefed mainsail.

G. A. Smith
DIMENSIONS OF SPARS
(in feet)

Spar	Fore	Main
Mast — deck to truck	94	96
Lower mast — deck to cap	64	66
Topmast	38	38
Boom	26½	57
Gaff	24½	25½
Jib-boom	34	

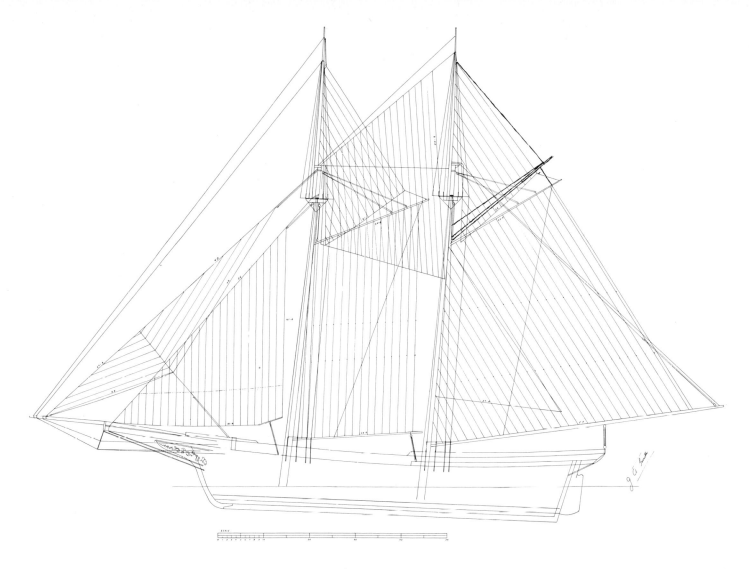

The G. A. Smith

Schooner   95 Tons
Built in 1884 at Lunenburg, N.S.,
by James Maxner.
82.8′ x 24.0′ x 8.9′

Sail plan: courtesy of Mr. Everett
Lohnes, Lunenburg, and Dalhousie
University Archives, Halifax, N.S.
Traced by Charles A. Armour.

An advertisement for the Marine Railway Company
from *Record of the Shipping of Yarmouth, N.S.*
by J. Murray Lawson, published in 1884.

Author's Collection.

The Woodboat

The woodboat was a type of vessel developed during the late eighteenth and nineteenth centuries along the lower reaches of the Saint John River. So-named because it was used primarily as a wood carrier, the vessel is almost certainly descended from the Chebacco-boat and the Dogbody of Massachusetts, with changes being made to suit local needs. These vessels had a full bow, broad beam and shallow draft, and had basically a schooner rig but without a bowsprit and headsails. This made them easy to handle in narrow creeks and shallow waters.

Before 1824 the shipping registers do not distinguish between woodboats and schooners. However, after the change in the format of the shipping register in 1824, the woodboats are described as schooners without a standing bowsprit. From then on it is possible to study the sizes and proportions of these vessels and to determine how many were built each year, although undoubtedly many of the smaller ones were not registered.

The list of Canadian shipping for 1873 lists 133 woodboats representing 8173 tons registered at Saint John. Most of these were built at Grand Lake, Long Reach and Canning, New Brunswick, and they ranged in size from 25 to over 100 tons. While owned and operated mainly by farmers and lumbermen on the Saint John River, many made regular trips along the Atlantic coast. They continued to be built until the early part of the twentieth century.

The spar plan of a woodboat (opposite) is unnamed and undated. Captain Robinson may have been the builder, owner or master. Both masts are gaff-rigged but do not carry topsails. Since there are no headsails or bowsprit, the foremast is stepped as far forward as possible.

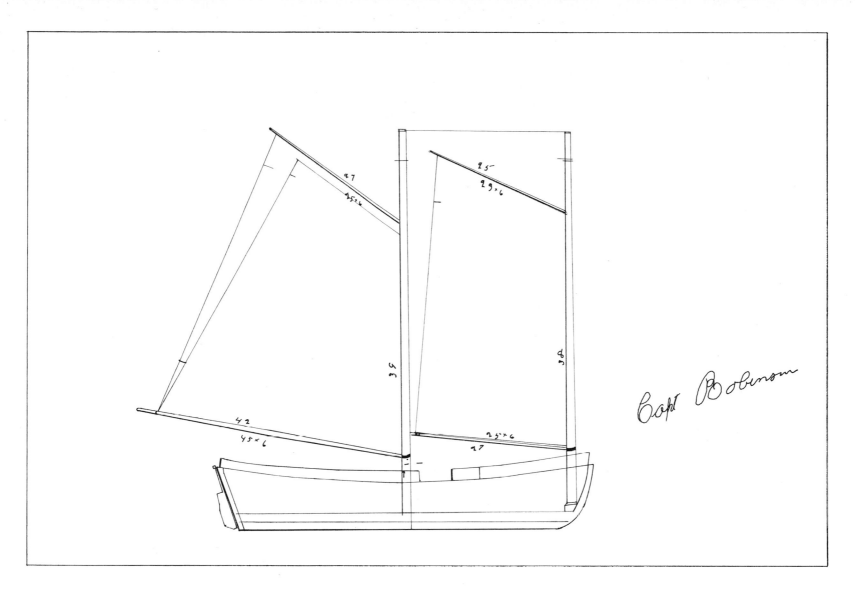

Woodboat

Original plan: courtesy of the
New Brunswick Museum, Saint John, N.B.
Traced by Thomas Lackey.

Two advertisements for Yarmouth businesses from *Record of the Shipping of Yarmouth*, N.S. by J. Murray Lawson, published in 1884.

The John M. Blaikie

Only two four-masted barques were built in the Maritimes and both were constructed in Nova Scotia. The first, the *John M. Blaikie* of 1778 tons, was built in 1885 at Great Village and named after her builder. The second, the *Kings County* of 2225 tons, was built at Kingsport by Ebenezer Cox in 1890 and owned by Charles R. Burgess.

The *John M. Blaikie* was partly owned by her builder and Archibald W. McLelan who at that time was Minister of Finance in Ottawa. The remaining shares were held by other members of the Blaikie and McLelan families. The vessel was wrecked in the Sunda Strait on May 4, 1892.

This painting shows the *John M. Blaikie* entering port and signaling for a pilot. The vessel is square-rigged on the fore, main and mizzen and carries courses, double topsails, double topgallants, royals and skysails. The fourth mast, or jigger, is fore-and-aft-rigged and carries a lower and upper spanker and a jigger topsail. The vessel's signal letters, W.K.N.D., are hoisted inferior to the Canadian Red Ensign being worn at the mizzen truck.

The John M. Blaikie

Barque   1778 Tons
Built in 1885 at Great Village, N.S.,
by John M. Blaikie.
245.2′ x 43.6′ x 24.0′

Oil on canvas.
By W. H. York, 1885.
Courtesy of the Public Archives
of Nova Scotia, Halifax, N.S.

The Habitant

The *Habitant*, a ship of 1618 tons launched in August of 1885, was the largest and last vessel built by Jonathan E. Steel at Scotts Bay for Stephen Sheffield and John Leander Wickwire. The association began in 1863 with the construction of the *J. Steel*, a barque of 568 tons. Over the next twenty-two years, Steel built six more barques, a ship and a brigantine for Sheffield and Wickwire.

The records[24] of Jonathan E. Steel indicate that the *Habitant* cost $37,058.80. However, the cost of rigging and outfitting the vessel was not included in this amount. The builder's cost accounts give interesting figures on labour costs, which varied depending on the time of year. Some examples are given below.

Daniel Legg			
Winter	54¾ days	$1.10	$ 60.22
Summer	116 days	1.45	168.20
Fall	41 days	1.31	53.71
Summer	93 days	1.45	134.85
			$416.98

Henry Thorpe	labour and board		
Winter	55 days	$1.10	$ 60.50
Summer	124½ days	1.55	192.97
Fall	48 days	1.40	67.20
Summer	130½ days	1.50	195.75
			$516.42

Henry Hudson			
Booring one side of ship			$247.50

J. E. Steel	oxen	111 days at 1.00	111.00
	horses	531½ days at 75¢	398.62

J. E. Steel	labour		
1st Winter	111 days	$1.50	$166.50
Summer	178½ days	2.50	446.25
Fall	63 days	2.35	148.05
Summer	129½ days	2.50	323.75
			$1084.55

William Butler	Labour and board		
Winter	77¾ days	$1.00	$ 77.75
Summer	109 days	1.50	163.50
Fall	45½ days	1.35	61.42
Logs at Steam Mill			37.46
Horse	7½ days	.75	5.62
			$ 345.75

Son Henry	Labour and Board		
Winter	35½ days	$0.80	$ 28.40
Summer	106¼ days	1.30	127.50
Fall	18¾ days	1.08	20.25
			$ 176.15

Wellington Sanford			
Job Booring and Driving Iron			$850.00

The *Habitant* was operated by Sheffield and Wickwire for ten years with many people, including the builder, owning shares. The ship had a very interesting career. She was sold in 1895, registered at Melbourne, Australia, and owned first by the Melbourne Shipping Company and later by the Melbourne Steamship Company. Some time before 1912, loaded with a cargo of petroleum, the vessel was gutted by fire while berthed at Melbourne. Later, the hull of the vessel was converted into a floating dry dock and remained in use until April 1958 when she was broken up and the timber used for firewood.

In this painting the vessel carries courses, double topsails, topgallants, and royals. The crossjack, skysails and the flying jib are being taken in.

The Habitant

Ship   1618 Tons
Built in 1885 at Scotts Bay, N.S.,
by Jonathan Steel.
225.0' x 42.7' x 24.0'

Oil on canvas.
By John Loos, 1887.
Courtesy of Mrs. Fred Huntley and
Miss Alice Wickwire, Kentville, N.S.

The County of Yarmouth

Ship   2154 Tons
Built in 1884 at Belleveau's Cove, N.S.,
by Hilaire P. Boudreau.
243.0′ x 44.5′ x 24.0′

Oil on canvas.
By Edward Adam, 1886.
Courtesy of the Yarmouth County
Historical Society, Yarmouth, N.S.

The County of Yarmouth

The *County of Yarmouth*, a ship of 2154 tons, holds the distinction of being the largest vessel built in the Yarmouth area. Launched on May 28, 1884, she was built at Belleveau's Cove by Hilaire P. Boudreau for William D. Lovitt. For many years the vessel traded regularly between Rio de Janeiro and British and Canadian ports.

On July 24, 1886, the *County of Yarmouth* arrived at North Sydney, Cape Breton, after a passage of 36 days from Rio de Janeiro. The vessel left Rio on June 18, crossed the equator on the 11th day out, passed Bermuda on the 30th day out, Cape Sable on the 34th day out, sighted Beaver Island light on the 35th day, and arrived at North Sydney the next day. The best day's run was 295 miles.

Seven years later, on October 10, 1893, the vessel was back at Sydney, and was chartered to load deal at Saint John for Liverpool. Shortly after leaving Sydney in ballast, the vessel dragged ashore on Petrics Ledges, Low Point, Cape Breton, during a gale, and filled with water. Early reports indicated that she would likely prove to be a total loss and that the vessel had been stripped, condemned and was to be sold at public auction. Later reports stated that the underwriters had contracted to float the ship.[25] Their efforts were successful and the vessel, after repairs at Halifax, continued to Saint John.

In December 1895 the vessel was dismasted and damaged at sea, towed into Grimsby, condemned and sold as a wreck to be broken up. However, she was subsequently sold to the Argentine Government to be used as a training ship.

By 1884 the number of ships and barques built was rapidly decreasing. After the *County of Yarmouth*, eight large ships, all of more than 1495 tons, were built in the Yarmouth area. In 1889 Israel L. Burrill built the *Jane Burrill* of 1835 tons at Little Brook and in the following year John R. Blanvelt built the last ship, the *J.Y. Robbins* of 1708 tons, at Tusket. A number of barques were also built, the last one being the *Mary A. Law* of 890 tons launched by John C. Blackader at Meteghan in 1890.

This painting shows the *County of Yarmouth* entering Havre on January 18, 1886. Her master was Thomas Corning. The vessel is running before the wind under shortened sail. She carries foresail, fore lower topsail, main lower topsail and jib. The ship's signal letters, J.N.H.G., are hoisted at the mizzen and the pilot jack at the foremast.

The Annie E. Wright

Ship   1847 Tons
Built in 1885 at Harvey, N.B.,
by Gaius S. Turner.
237.9' x 43.0' x 24.2'

Oil on canvas.
By Edward Adam, 1892.
Courtesy of the New Brunswick
Museum, Saint John, N.B.

The Annie E. Wright

Apart from giving full coverage of the launching of vessels, the local newspapers often gave glowing accounts of the builders and owners and their contribution to the community. A typical example apeared in the *Daily Times*, Moncton, New Brunswick, on Monday, June 15, 1885.

The steamer "Ripple's excursion to Harvey has been rather disappointing, no doubt, to those on board. She reached Harvey on Saturday in good time, notwithstanding the gale, but found that the big ship would not be launched till Monday (to-day). The excursionists started to return to Moncton but owing to the adverse wind did not reach here until last night. This handsome ship is the largest ever built in Albert County. . . .
The best of black bay-shore spruce has been used in her construction besides oak, pitch pine, birch, etc. She has ample accomodations for sailors, while the officers' rooms are airy and commodious. She is fastened with copper and galvanized iron and is fitted with all the modern improvements, including a patent "wild cat" windlass.
J. Nelson Smith, Esq., of Coverdale, is one of the principal owners, though Capt. Wright, who commands her, and others have shares in her.
This makes the twelfth vessel built by Hon. Mr. Turner at the "Bank shipyard" since 1875. . . .
The construction of this fleet of ships has created a vast amount of business and given employment to many men, and the County of Albert certainly owes a deep debt of gratitude to Mr. Turner for the incalculable benefit his enterprize has proven to it.
We cannot close this hasty sketch without a reference to the master builder of all these ships. C.F. Dow. Esq. He is thoroughly master of his business and these 12 vessels are monuments of his skill, no finer specimens of the shipbuilders craft being found in the Dominion of Canada.

More news was published two days later.

Mr. Turner's Big ship, the "Annie E. Wright" was launched at Harvey Bank on Monday and arrived at St. John on Tuesday morning, in tow of the "G.D. Hunter". The run down was made inside of thirteen hours, which is pretty fast travelling. The "Annie" is a magnificent ship, gracefully proportioned and substantially built.

The *Annie E. Wright* was registered at Dorchester on July 21, 1885, with John Nelson Smith as the managing owner. Her master was George Wright. On June 26, 1897, just over twelve years from her launching, the vessel was condemned and sold in Saint John. She was purchased and later repaired by Joseph K. Dunlop, registered at Saint John on September 28, 1897 and renamed *Madras*.

The *Madras* left Saint John with a cargo of deals and on October 22, 1897, while docking at Sharpness, England, in charge of a pilot and tug boat, ". . . got out of her course owing to a sudden dense fog . . ."[26] stranded, and became a total loss.

The *Annie E. Wright* is shown in this painting under full sail. The ship's signal letters, K.B.N.Q., have been hoisted inferior to the Red Ensign worn at the monkey gaff.

The Abyssinia

Photographs of deck scenes and interior shots of cabins are both extremely rare. The photograph on the left was taken from the roof of the after cabin looking forward. The spanker boom can be seen overhead. The large sail is the mainsail and in front of this can be seen the sheet of the mizzen staysail. On the left the old sailmaker is busy at work repairing a sail while another member of the crew is facing the camera.

The *Abyssinia*, a barque of 1127 tons, was built at Saint John, New Brunswick in 1885 by Oliver Pittfield. The vessel remained in the Taylor Brothers fleet until 1904 when she was sold to Italian subjects. She was still afloat in 1920.

The photograph on the right is an interior shot of the captain's cabin. The woman is the wife of Arthur W. Hilton, master of the *Abyssinia* from 1889 to 1904, and the child is their daughter. On the left is a reed organ, a popular musical instrument of the period. A painting of the *Abyssinia* hangs on the wall and an assortment of family photographs on the shelf give the cabin a homelike atmosphere.

The Abyssinia—deck scene

Courtesy of the Yarmouth County
Historical Society, Yarmouth, N.S.

The Abyssinia—captain's cabin

Barque   1127 Tons
Built in 1885 at Saint John, N.B.,
by Oliver Pittfield.
186.5′ x 36.7′ x 22.4′

The Hilaria

On July 31, 1886, the *Hilaria*, a ship of 1675 tons, was launched from the yard of Joseph K. Dunlop. She was the last square-rigger to be built in Saint John. Four years later, Dunlop launched his last vessel, the *Curler*, a barque of 807 tons. This vessel and the *Sayre* of 706 tons, launched a few months earlier, were the last two barques built in the city.

From 1873 until 1877 Joseph Kidd Dunlop built seven ships, all over 1400 tons, for James Hamilton Moran at Saint John. The largest of these, and the largest of his vessels, was the *Prince Waldemar*, a ship of 1696 tons built in 1876. After Moran's death in 1877, Dunlop built two more ships and four more barques for William Thomson & Company of Saint John.

Born in 1818 in Dundee, Scotland, William Thomson came to Saint John with his parents. He began as a ship broker and in 1850 owned his first vessel, the *British Queen*, a brigantine of 125 tons, which had been built at Digby in 1848. In the late 1850s and early 1860s he owned a number of vessels in partnership with William Wright, Jacob Troop and Zebedee Ring, but later owned and operated his own vessels. His sons Robert and John took over the firm when William retired in 1882. The company owned one of the largest fleets of vessels in Saint John and, like the Troops, purchased a number of steel sailing ships which they operated until the early part of the twentieth century.

The *Hilaria* was owned and operated by the Thomsons for nine years. On July 9, 1895, the vessel was burnt at Melbourne, Australia.

This sail plan of the *Hilaria* is by George E. Holder, one of the most prominent sailmakers in Saint John. His company supplied the sails for many well-known builders and owners, not only in Saint John and Yarmouth, but in other ports along the Bay of Fundy coast. His son William took over the business and was the last of the old sailmakers in Saint John. The company is still in operation today under the name of George E. Holder and Son.

This plan shows clearly the standing rigging of a ship of the late nineteenth century and the arrangement of the double topsails and double topgallants. The vessel had no jib boom. The jibs were carried on a spike bowsprit.

Hilaria
DIMENSIONS OF SPARS
(in feet)

Spar	Fore	Main	Mizzen
Mast — deck to truck	138	144	120
Lower mast — deck to cap	56	62	55
Topmast	52	52	43½
Topgallant and royal	54	54	43
Lower yard	84	84	69
Lower topmast yard	74	74	62
Upper topmast yard	69	69	57
Lower topgallant yard	62	62	50
Upper topgallant yard	57	57	45
Royal yard	45	45	37
Spanker boom			60
Bowsprit	48		

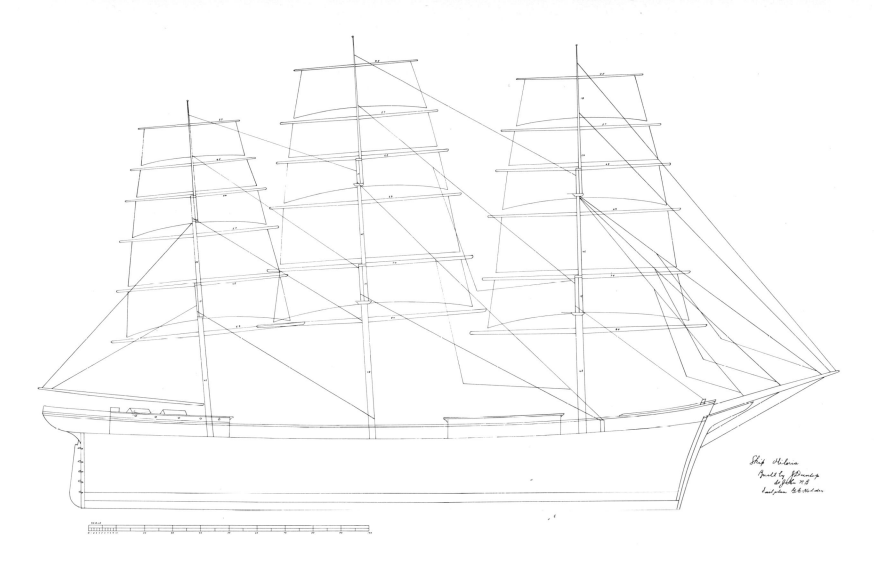

The Hilaria

Ship   1675 Tons
Built in 1886 at Saint John, N.B.,
by Joseph K. Dunlop.
225.0′ x 41.0′ x 24.0′

Original sail plan: courtesy of the
New Brusnwick Museum, Saint John, N.B.
Traced by Thomas Lackey &
Charles A. Armour.

The Skoda

The highlight of the building of any vessel was, of course, the launching day. Many launchings were witnessed only by the builders, but the launching of a large vessel might attract several thousand people and be accompanied by picnics, banquets or bazaars.

The following comment on launching festivities appeared in the *Saint John Daily News*, Saturday, September 9, 1876.

> They have a pleasant practice up the Bay of going from far and near to launches, the number of ships built not lessening the popular interest in this respect. Taking advantage of this fact, the organizers of church and charity bazaars and tea meetings have them on launch days. At the launch of the bark CALCUTTA, at Spencer's Island, a few days ago, there were people from Mill Village, Windsor, and other places on both sides of the Bay present, and the bazaar netted $248 for a place of worship to be open to ministers of all denominations.

In some cases there were accidents. Occasionally the vessel stuck on the ways or people were injured. Some mishaps were more humiliating than tragic, especially if the vessel got away and fetched up in the mud bank on the opposite shore. This, in fact, happened quite frequently. If the tide fell, however, and the vessel dropped over on her side, the results could be disastrous.

This contemporary photograph shows the launching of the *Skoda*, a barquentine of 658 tons built by Ebenezer Cox at Kingsport, Nova Scotia, in 1893 for Rufus Burgess. Under the bow can be seen the cradle on which the vessel rests. The cradle in turn slides on the launching ways, visible on the left. The large vessel in the background is the ship *Canada*.

The launching of the *Skoda* marked the end of thirty years of shipbuilding for Ebenezer Cox. Cox had begun designing and building vessels for Joseph E. Woodworth in 1864 when he built the *Diadem*, a schooner of 91 tons. From 1869 until 1876 most of their vessels were built for Charles W. Bertaux, a merchant from New York.

When Woodworth retired in 1876 the yard was taken over by Peter R. Crichton, and Cox remained as the master builder. Over the next seventeen years they built fifteen vessels. Most of these, barques and ships over a thousand tons, were built for C. Rufus Burgess of Wolfville. Four of their barques were built for William Thomson of Saint John. After 1882 they built eight more vessels for Burgess, four of which were over two thousand tons. The two largest of these were the *Kings County*, a four-masted barque of 2225 tons built in 1890 and the *Canada*, a ship of 2301 tons built in 1891.

The *Skoda* was owned by Burgess until 1900 when the registered owners became the Barquentine Skoda Company Limited of Wolfville. In 1912 the vessel was sold to Lester Ashley Rodden of Mobile, Alabama, and registered at that port in 1915.

The Skoda

Barquentine   658 Tons
Built in 1893 at Kingsport, N.S.,
by Ebenezer Cox.   Courtesy of Mr. Scott M.
168.0′ x 37.0′ x 16.0′   Blenkhorn, Canning, N.S.

The Strathern

Courtesy of the Dalhousie University
Archives, Halifax, N.S.

This photograph of the *Strathern*, moored at a dock, gives a wealth of rigging and deck detail. The sails are furled on the yards and the royal, topgallant and upper topsail yards are shown in the lowered position. The location of the deck houses and lifeboats can be clearly seen. Just in front of the mizzen mast, beside the lifeboat, is a wind-driven pump.

The *Strathern*, a barque of 1373 tons, was built at Maitland, Nova Scotia, in 1893 by Joseph Montieth for Alfred Putman. In May 1908 the vessel became waterlogged and was abandoned at sea.

Newcastle, N.B. Barque careened on the river bank

Courtesy of the Provincial Archives
of New Brunswick, Fredericton, N.B.

This method of exposing the bottom of a vessel for repairs or cleaning has been used for centuries. Heavy tackles have been attached to the lower mastheads and secured to the bank. Tightening these tackles will heel the vessel to the desired angle so that the necessary work can be carried out.

This method had to be used in areas where dry dock facilities were not available. To facilitate the operation and avoid damage to the spars and rigging, the upper yards have been removed and the topgallant and royal masts on the fore and main have been struck.

The Atrato

Born in 1822, John MacLeod began building at Liverpool, Nova Scotia, in 1845 and continued for another twenty-eight years. His son Robie took over the yard when his father and brother were lost at sea in August of 1873. From 1875 until he retired in 1920, he not only designed his own vessels, but designed vessels for other builders as well. In 1893, in a competition sponsored by the Department of Marine and Fisheries, Robie won the first prize of $400 "for the best model of a fishing and freight carrying schooner."[27]

One of his best-known vessels, noted for her speed and fine lines, was the *Howard D. Troop*, a schooner of 69 tons built in 1896 and for many years a pilot boat in Saint John. On August 12, 1897 he launched the *Atrato* of 199 tons, one of a number of topsail schooners that he built. The vessel was owned by W. and C. H. Mitchell of Halifax and for many years was engaged in the fruit trade between New York and the West Indies. An excellent description of the vessel, written by G. B. Douglas, appeared in *The Rudder* magazine in April 1901:

> . . . Built of hard and soft woods mixed, galvanized iron and copper-fastened, sheathed with yellow metal and salted. Her speed is from 42 to 44 knots in four hours under favorable conditions.
>
> Her first port of call is Bocas del Toro, in the United States of Colombia, the run being made in about twenty days from New York; thence to Colon and Cartagena. At the latter port she has to ask permission to trade on the coast. She is compelled to take a Custom House Officer along with her to the San Blas coast, where the trading for cocoanuts is done, board him and pay his fare back home again. She may keep him on board some six weeks, and if he happens to be an objectionable person, he is not very good company for the captain to have on board, and he is generally glad to get rid of him and be off to New York, where he arrives after an absence of about four months.
>
> The trading is all done with regular dealers, who in turn trade with the Indians or natives, who gather and bring the nuts to the coast in their canoes or small sail boats. . . . Four hundred thousand cocoanuts comprised the cargo at the time I visited the Atrato.
>
> . . . .
>
> Her crew consist of captain, two mates, a cook and four sailors, or if Indians are carried, eight of them are necessary to do the work of the four whites
>
> . . . .
>
> The cabin was of ample size, the bulkheads and doors being of oak, in the natural finish, the capitals of the columns being done with gold leaf and the ceiling painted with ample skylights and ports, making a very comfortable and roomy place.

On January 14, 1905, the vessel was dismasted and stranded on the coast of British Honduras. She was later got off, repaired and registered at Belize in January 1906. On December 10, while on a voyage from Philadelphia to St. John's, Newfoundland, loaded with coal, she put into Liverpool for shelter during a snowstorm and at 11 P.M. struck on Neils Ledge and became a total loss.

The photograph shows the *Atrato* in New York Harbour. At a quick glance, the vessel could be mistaken for a brigantine; however, she carried a fore-and-aft sail on the foremast. Her rig was unusual in that she set a sail on the lower yard and also carried a topgallant sail.

The Atrato

Topsail Schooner   199 Tons
Built in 1897 at Liverpool, N.S.,
by Robie MacLeod.
107.6′ x 27.5′ x 10.6′

MARKET SLIPP LOW WATER

Saint John, N.B. Market Slip at low water

Courtesy of the Provincial Archives
of New Brunswick, Fredericton, N.B.

The Bay of Fundy has some of the world's highest tides. The tidal range at Saint John varies between twenty and twenty-eight feet. This late nineteenth century photograph shows the market slip at low water. A variety of small vessels rest on the mud. The scow in the foreground is loaded with barrels of dried fish. Horse-drawn sloven waggons are being used to transfer the barrels.

Saint John, N.B. Market Slip at high water

Courtesy of the Provincial Archives
of New Brunswick, Fredericton, N.B.

Although taken many years later, this view shows the same scene at high tide. The vessel on the right is the *Leonice*, a schooner of 27 tons, built as the *Quick Step* at Gloucester, Massachusetts, in 1856 and registered at Saint Andrew's, New Brunswick, in 1908.

In 1916 she was placed on the Halifax register and two years later an auxiliary engine was installed. Directly astern is the *Wanita*, a schooner of 42 tons built at Granville, Nova Scotia by Joseph Healy in 1897.

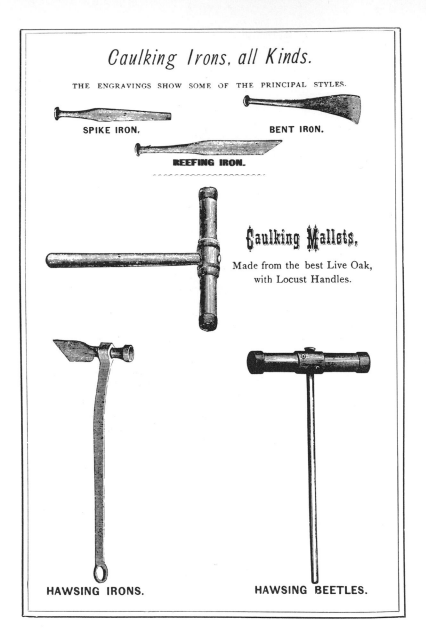

From the J. Snelling & Co.
*Catalogue of Ship, Steamboat
and Yacht Fixtures*, New York, 1874.

Courtesy of the
Dalhousie University Archives,
Halifax, N.S.

Shipbuilders' Tools and Rigging Gear

Tools used by shipbuilders have changed very little for many centuries. Those found on board the *Vasa* (1628) are very similar to ones in use three hundred years later.

A selection of shipbuilders' tools and rigging gear is found on the right.

1., 2. Caulking mallet and caulking iron, respectively. These were used for driving oakum into the seams of the hull after the hull had been planked.
3. Broadaxe.
4. Serving mallet and reel.
5. Small serving mallet used by a sailmaker.
6. Auger — for boring holes in wood.
7. Wooden block plane.
8. Wooden mould plane.
9. Wooden mallet.
10. Adze — a tool similar to an axe with an arched blade at right angles to the handle.
11. Fid — a wooden taper for forcing the strands of rope apart when splicing.
12. Sailor's palm — used by sailmakers when forcing needles through heavy canvas (really an adaptation of the thimble).
13. Large set of dividers used for measuring off distances.
14. Heart — used in rigging for setting up stays.
15. Wooden rigging block — the grooves in the side are for the rope strop.
16. Bevel — used for setting off angles.

Shipbuilders' tools and rigging gear

Courtesy of the Nova Scotia
Museum, Halifax, N.S., and
the Author's Collection.

Revival 1901-1925

By the beginning of the twentieth century most of the large ocean-going sailing ships had been driven from the foreign trade by the steamship. The Maritimes, however, had an extensive local and foreign coastal trade which had been carried out in small brigantines and schooners. Even after the introduction of the railways and up until the establishment of a good road transport system, most of the local trade around the coast was done in small schooners. Extensive foreign coastal trade with the United States, the West Indies and South America had been carried on for over a century and a half.

The principal exports from the Maritimes, especially New Brunswick and Nova Scotia, were timber, fish, gypsum and, to a much lesser extent, coal. In return, salt, molasses and rum were imported from the West Indies, and hard coal, hard pine and manufactured goods from the United States. These trades were not affected to a great extent by the rivalry of steam. The fore-and-aft rigs had always been very profitable for coastal navigation. They were easy to handle, manoeuvrable in narrow channels and rivers and economical to operate.

The outbreak of war in 1914 and the subsequent heavy losses to Allied shipping resulted in increased freight rates and a sudden demand for vessels of all descriptions. By 1916 the building boom was well under way and continued until after the war. In the peak years from 1917 to 1920, nearly 300 three- and four-masted schoon-

ers were built as well as hundreds of small ones. After the war the shipbuilding programs of many countries rapidly produced many large steamers, and normal trade patterns were reestablished. While the small schooners were still used extensively for the fishing industry, the large schooners were no longer commercially viable and gradually disappeared from the scene.

As might be expected, the period of the twentieth century is by far the easiest to study. Many of the companies are still operating and their records are extant. Many of the builders, owners, crew members, shipwrights and sailmakers are still alive. Plans and half-models are available and, while there are few paintings, there are countless photographs. All of these allow a detailed study of hull design, rigging changes and deck and cabin layouts. Building tools of the late nineteenth and early twentieth centuries can be found in many museums, private collections and antique shops throughout the Maritime Provinces.

The shipbuilding tradition, however, did not disappear entirely, especially in Nova Scotia. Fishing schooners, now fitted with auxiliary engines, continued to be built mainly in Lunenburg and Meteghan until the 1940s. One of the last of the salt bankers was the *Theresa E. Connor*, a schooner of 91 tons built at Lunenburg in 1938 by Smith and Rhuland. This vessel has now been restored and is a floating museum at Lunenburg.

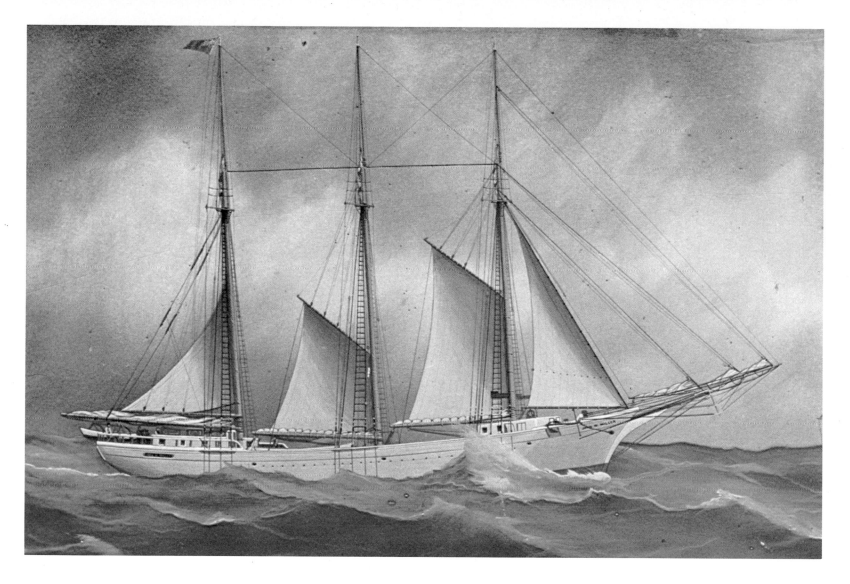

The John W. Miller

Tern schooner   266 Tons
Built in 1918 at Mahone Bay, N.S.,
by McLean Construction Co., Ltd.
122.5′ x 30.5′ x 11.6′

Gouache.
Unsigned and undated.
Courtesy of the Nova Scotia
Museum, Halifax, N.S.

LUNENBURG MARINE RAILWAY,
LUNENBURG, N. S.

NO. 1 RAILWAY.   CAPACITY 400 TONS.
NO. 2 RAILWAY.   "   500   "

Courtesy of the
Dalhousie University Archives,
Halifax, Nova Scotia.

This simple method for hauling vessels out of the water for repairs was used extensively and marine railways were found in many ports. The vessel rests in a cradle which in turn runs on a railway track. The Lunenburg Marine Railway was built around 1900 and the company is still in operation.

The John W. Miller

The *John W. Miller* was registered at Lunenburg in October 1918, and owned by John C. Crosbie of St. John's, Newfoundland. In December of the same year the registration was transferred to Newfoundland and the vessel was employed in the Brazil trade for many years. On November 28, 1930, she sailed from Newfoundland with a cargo of 4925 drums of salt fish bound for Bahia and Pernambuco. Shortly afterwards the vessel ran into heavy weather and started to leak. She was abandoned at sea on December 30, and the crew were taken off by the German steamer *Wido*.

The *John W. Miller* is shown here in a storm under reduced canvas. The fore staysail (or jumbo) has been set. There is a single reef in the foresail and a double reef in the main. The spanker has been furled and replaced by a storm trysail.

Lunenburg

A tern schooner and a large number of two-masted schooners lie at anchor in the harbour. In the foreground is the building yard of Smith and Rhuland, established in 1900. On the left a schooner is undergoing repairs on the Marine Railway. To the far right, a new schooner is nearing completion. The seams are being caulked and puttied and preparations for launching are underway.

Between the two schooners another vessel is under construction. The keel has been laid, the stern post is in position and one of the frames is secured to it. Six frames, which have been carefully cut to take the natural curve of the wood, are lying on the framing stage. A large quantity of curved lumber, to be used for the rest of the frames, lies on the ground. The photograph shows clearly the small space required to build a vessel.

Lunenburg Harbour, c. 1905

Courtesy of Mr. Walter K. Morrison,
Lawrencetown, Annapolis County, N.S.

The Half-Model

The first step in the construction of a vessel was the carving of the half-model, often done by the master builder. While the scale of the half-model varied from builder to builder, the model represented accurately the shape of half of the hull to the outside of the frames. The models were usually made of layers of wood joined together by screws or wooden pegs. These layers represented the various water lines and sheer lines of the vessel.

Once the half-model was completed, the lines were taken off. Often the half-model was taken apart and the shapes of the individual layers were then traced onto a piece of paper. In other cases, perpendiculars were dropped from the water lines to a piece of paper to give the shape of the hull. This gave the familiar sheer and profile and half-breadth plan. Lines called "vertical stations" were drawn across the model at right angles to the keel. In some cases, especially for small vessels, no plans were prepared. The width of the layers of the half-model were measured at each vertical station and a table of offsets was prepared. Working directly from the drawings or from a table of offsets, and applying the appropriate scale, the shape of the frames at any position was plotted and drawn on the mould-loft floor. The mould loft itself had a smooth clean floor which was wooden-pegged so that the lines of one vessel could be easily planed off before another was laid down. The centre line, or keel, was marked along one edge of the floor and the shape of each frame was also drawn on the floor. Light wooden moulds were then made and used as templates for the construction of the frames.

The frames were constructed on the framing stage, a platform flush with the top of the keel extending from stem to sternpost. As the frames were assembled they were raised and secured to the keel.

This photograph shows the half-model of the *Oressa Bell*. Directly below is the half-breadth plan, and the bottom drawing is the sheer and profile. The *Oressa Bell*, a schooner of 95 tons, was built at Mahone Bay in 1903 by David Burgoyne. The vessel was registered at Lunenburg and was owned by a group of merchants and mariners of Mahone Bay until 1921 when she was sold to mariners from Newfoundland. On November 29, 1919, the *Oressa Bell* was driven ashore on the coast of Newfoundland and became a total loss.

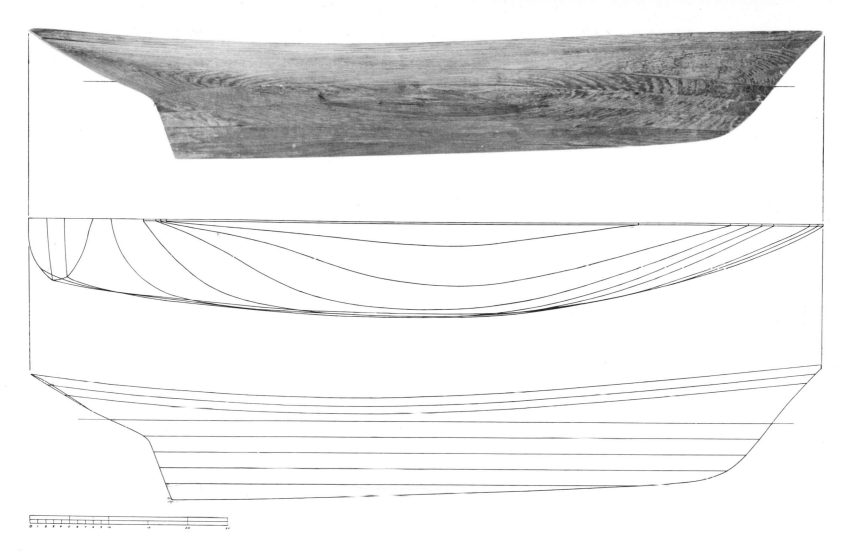

The Oressa Belle

Schooner   95 Tons
Built in 1903 at Mahone Bay, N.S.,
by David E. Burgoyne.
89.6′ x 25.0′ x 9.5′

Half model: courtesy of the
Nova Scotia Museum, Halifax, N.S.
Lines taken off by Charles A. Armour
Drawing prepared by Ian MacKay.

Montague, P.E.I.

The three-masted schooner is the *Empress*, 335 tons, built at Montague in 1901 by George W. Wightman and owned by the builder. In the foreground, a small vessel is being planked. On the opposite shore, another vessel is in frame.

The Sceptre icing to wharf, Lunenburg, N.S.

Courtesy of Mr. Telene Gray,
La Have, N.S.

The *Sceptre*, a brigantine of 142 tons, was built at Lunenburg in 1887 by David Smith and owned by Zwicker & Company for twenty-five years. During this time she was engaged in the West Indies trade and on one occasion completed the voyage from Lunenburg to the West Indies and back in twenty-six days, a record for the period. On September 13, 1912, while on a voyage to the West Indies, the vessel collided with the British steamer *Roseland* and sank. The crew were saved by the steamer.

This photograph was taken in 1905 after the *Sceptre* had arrived at Lunenburg with a cargo of salt from Turks Island. A channel to the wharf is being cut through the ice.

The A. V. Conrad

As we have seen, a number of three-masted schooners (or tern schooners as they were later called) had been built in the Maritimes as early as 1814 and the rig was not uncommon during the mid-nineteenth century. Since no plans or illustrations of these early types have survived, it is not known whether any of these carried square topsails. The rig became popular in the years following the decline of the square-rig sailing ships and a large number were built during the first decade of the twentieth century. During the peak years of building, 1918 to 1919, more than 150 were launched.

The smallest tern schooner was the *Effie Howard* of 24 tons built by James Verge at Sheet Harbour in 1902. Originally fitted with two masts, the vessel was rebuilt in 1911 at Pugwash by Daniel Henderson and converted to a three-master. The largest tern schooner was the *Gypsum Princess* of 664 tons built by D. S. Howard at Parrsboro in 1892.

The last cargo-carrying three-masted schooner was the *Mary B. Brooks* of 214 tons. Building was started in 1920 by W. D. Foley at Plympton, Nova Scotia, but stopped when the vessel was in frame. Work was resumed five years later under new owners. After yet another change in ownership, the vessel was finally completed in 1926. The Royal Canadian Navy built the *Venture*, a three-masted schooner of 170 tons at Meteghan, Nova Scotia, in 1938 and she was used for a short time as a training ship.

The first four-masted schooner constructed in the Maritimes was the *Uruguay* of 726 tons built by Shubael Dimock at Windsor in 1889. Three more were built in 1892. However, it was not until World War I that the rig was extensively used and twenty were built in 1918 and 1919.

Many of the larger four-masters were built along the Minas Basin shore. In 1918 Fauquier and Porter built the *Margaret F.*

Dick of 989 tons and the *Jessie Louise Fauquier* of 939 tons, both at Hantsport, the two largest of this type to be built in the Maritimes. In the same year, W. R. Huntley built the *Governor Parr* of 912 tons at Parrsboro and George Wagstaff built the *Frieda E.* of 669 tons at Port Greville. The following year saw the launching of the *George Melville Cochran* of 820 tons built by George M. Cochran at Port Greville, and in 1920 W. R. Huntley launched the *Whitebell* of 572 tons, the last four-master to be built.

The *A. V. Conrad* of 147 tons represents one of the many small three-masted schooners constructed in the Maritimes. The vessel was built by Melbourne Leary in 1908 at La Have, Nova Scotia, and named after the owner. She was later owned by A. E. Hickman of St. John's, Newfoundland. In February, 1921, while on a voyage from Cadiz to Newfoundland with a cargo of salt, the vessel was abandoned in a derelict condition and the crew were picked up by an Italian passenger liner.

The sail plan of the *A. V. Conrad*, by Harry Ham of Lunenburg, shows clearly the positions of the masts, spars and sails of a tern schooner. The location of the forward house and after cabin are also indicated.

A. V. Conrad
DIMENSIONS OF SPARS
(in feet)

Spar	Fore	Main	Mizzen
Mast — deck to truck	89	91	92
Lower mast — deck to cap	59	61	62
Topmast	38	38	38
Boom	25'10"	25'6"	40
Gaff	24	24'6"	31'6"
Jib-boom	31'6"		

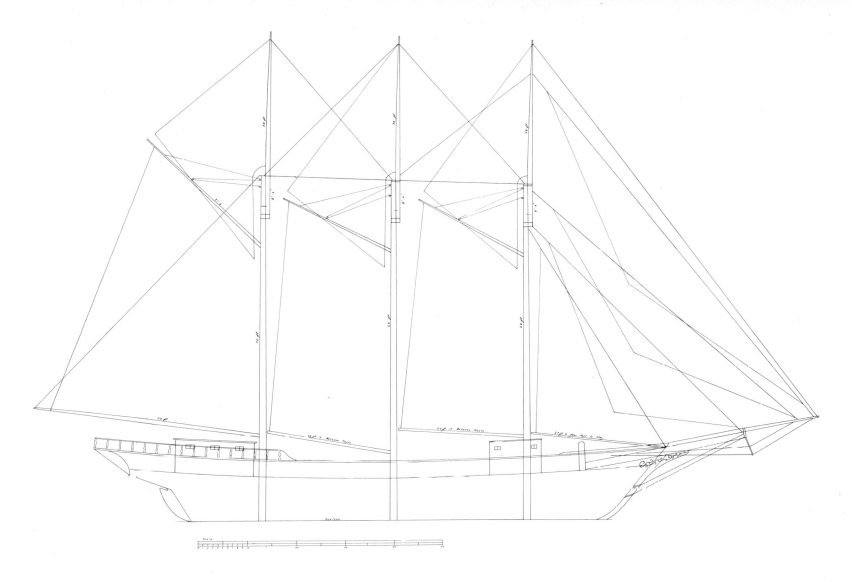

The A. V. Conrad

Tern schooner   147 Tons
Built in 1908 at La Have, N.S.,
by Melbourne Leary.
101.6′ x 27.2′ x 10.0′

Sail plan: courtesy of Mr. Everett
Lohnes, Lunenburg, and Dalhousie
University Archives, Halifax, N.S.
Traced by Charles A. Armour.

Montague, P.E.I., after 1907

Courtesy of the Public Archives
of Prince Edward Island,
Charlottetown, P.E.I.

Eight schooners are moored in the harbour. Two of these carry only a topmast on the main. The third vessel from the left is the *Grace Darling*, a schooner of 100 tons built at Mahone Bay in 1902 and registered at Lunenburg. The small vessel on her port side is the *Silver Spray*, a schooner of 16 tons built at Montague in 1907 and registered at Charlottetown.

Fishermen at Souris, P.E.I., c.1910

Two fishing schooners are moored at the wharf. The deck of the vessel in the foreground is littered with fishing gear. The compionway in the stern, forward of the wheel, and the forward companionway both lead to the crew's accommodations.

Jacob Whitman Raymond

When Jacob Whitman Raymond launched the *Breakers*, a four-masted schooner of 517 tons, in August 1918, he was seventy-five years old and the occasion marked the end of nearly sixty years of shipbuilding. His father, Eleazer Raymond, had begun building at Port Maitland in the mid-1850s and the young Raymond assisted his father in the construction of the *Renfrew*, a brigantine of 90 tons launched in 1860. Two years later he was made foreman of his father's yard and in 1864 they launched their first ship, the *Mary Raymond* of 678 tons. Their largest vessel was the *Emily L. Boyd*, a barque of 1240 tons launched in 1881.

In 1884 J. Whitman Raymond went to the United States and for nearly twenty years designed yachts for a number of Massachusetts builders, including Lawley's of Boston. He returned briefly to Nova Scotia between 1889 and 1892 and, assisted by his father, superintended the construction of five schooners for J. William Smith of Saint John.

With the revival of shipbuilding during World War I, Raymond again returned to Nova Scotia. In 1917 he superintended the construction of the *Socony*, a tern schooner of 314 tons built by Innocent Comeau at Little Brook for Frederick M. Jones. Whitman built three more tern schooners and a large number of small schooners before launching the *Breakers* in 1919.

This photograph shows the *Socony* on the launchways at Little Brook. The masts have just been stepped and the shrouds are being set up. The vessel was registered at Weymouth, immediately sold to James A. Urquhart, a merchant in St. John's, Newfoundland, and, in November, was sold to the Standard Transportation Company Limited of Hong Kong. On February 26, 1919, while on a voyage from St. Ann's, Jamaica, to New York, she was stranded on the south coast of the Isle of Pines in the Caribbean Sea and became a total loss. The loss, including the cargo, was estimated at $160,000.

The Socony

Tern schooner   314 Tons
Built in 1917 at Little Brook, N.S.,
by J. Whitman Raymond.
132.0′ x 31.9′ x 11.9′

Courtesy of Mr. Clifford Hardy,
North Pembroke, Mass.

The construction of the Dornfontein

This sequence of photographs shows the construction of the *Dornfontein*, a four-masted schooner of 695 tons built by the Marine Construction Company Canada Limited at Portland, New Brunswick, in 1918.

NOVEMBER 5, 1917 — The above photograph shows the vessel in an early stage of building. The keel has been laid and the sternpost on the right is in position. Ten sets of double frames are up and have been secured to the keel; another set is being raised into position. The men are working on a framing stage. The frames are supported by long poles called bilge shores.

JANUARY 29, 1918 — This view, taken from the bow, shows the vessel in frame and the deck beams in position. Under the bow can be seen the keel blocks on which the vessel rests. The black batten, four feet below the top of the frames, represents the vessel's sheer line. The men will start planking from the sheer line and work downwards; and from the garboard (the plank next to the keel) and work upwards, meeting near the middle.

MAY 7, 1918 — The deck has been laid, the deck houses are in position and the planking is nearing completion. The frames are still visible on the turn of the bilge where planking has not been finished. As the vessel was planked, the seams were caulked with oakum, usually puttied, and the hull painted. Fifty-seven men are shown in the photograph.

The dimensions of the vessel were: 171.7′ x 40.1′ x 17.9′.

The *Dornfontein* was registered at Saint John on July 8, 1918, and owned by the builder. This photograph shows the *Dornfontein* loaded and being towed out to sea. She carries a very large deck-load of heavy timber. The funnel of the tug is just visible behind the jigger mast. The vessel had a very short life. On August 2, 1918, she was burnt by a German submarine off Brier Island in the Bay of Fundy. The crew survived.

Liverpool, N.S.

Courtesy of Mr. Hector
MacLeod, Liverpool, N.S.

Liverpool, Nova Scotia

Scenes like this were common in many ports in the Maritime Provinces up until the 1920s. This photograph was taken in Liverpool, Nova Scotia, before 1912. The vessels are loading timber from flatcars.

Three tern schooners are shown in the foreground. The schooner next to the wharf is the *Georgina Roop* of 424 tons, built at Granville Ferry by Pickels and Mills in 1906. The schooner in the middle is the *Laura* of 299 tons, built at Liverpool, Nova Scotia, in 1901 by Jason Gardner. The *Laura* was transferred to Bridgetown, Barbados, in 1912. The *Georgina Roop* was sailing under the Russian flag in 1920 as the *Pineland*.

The Maid of England

The photograph on the right shows the building crew of the *Maid of England*, a barquentine of 696 tons built at Grosses Coques, Nova Scotia in 1919 by Omer Blinn. This was the last square-rigged vessel built in the Maritimes. The majority of the workmen are old men, an indication of the fact that by this time the number of skilled shipwrights was diminishing.

The half-model of the *Maid of England* was cut by W. R. Huntley, a well-known shipbuilder of Parrsboro. The model was also used for the construction of the *Cumberland Queen*, a four-masted schooner of 634 tons built at Diligent River in 1919 by Robinson and Pugsley.

The *Maid of England* was owned by Frank K. Warren of Halifax for nine years. She was abandoned at sea in 1928.

The building crew of the Maid of England

Barquentine   690 Tons
Built in 1919 at Grosses Coques, N.S.,
by Omer Blinn.
174.7′ x 37.6′ x 13.0′

The Bluenose and the Canadia

The *Bluenose* is without doubt the most famous of the vessels built in Nova Scotia. The first vessel by this name was the *Blue Nose*, a schooner of 56 tons built at Lunenburg in 1850 by Elkanah Zwicker. The name remained fairly popular, and several other vessels with this name were built in the Maritimes.

The first Nova Scotia Fleet Race, held in 1920, was won by the *Delawana* which was, in turn, defeated by the *Esperanto* in the International Series off Halifax later that year. In the following year the *Bluenose*, skippered by Angus Walters, competed in the Nova Scotia Fleet Race against seven other Nova Scotia vessels including the *Delawana* and the *Canadia* and won both races. On October 22 and 24 she raced against the *Elsie* of Gloucester and won the International Championship.

In 1922 *Bluenose* again represented Nova Scotia in the International Series and beat the *Henry Ford* of Gloucester. In the following year the *Bluenose* defeated the *Columbia* in two successive races off Halifax. However, after the second race, Ben Pine, master of the *Columbia*, claimed the *Bluenose* had taken a marker on the wrong side. The protest was upheld and the race was declared void. Walters claimed the marker was not within the course and indignantly took the *Bluenose* back to Lunenburg.

In 1930 *Bluenose* raced against the *Gertrude L. Thebauld* off Gloucester for the Lipton Cup and lost both races. In 1931 *Bluenose* accepted the challenge from the Americans for the International Series and defeated the *Thebauld* in the first two races. Seven years later, in 1938, another International Series was held off Gloucester and the two vessels met for the last time. *Bluenose* lost the first race, won the second and third and lost the fourth. On October 26, 1938, in one of the most exciting races of her career, *Bluenose* defeated the *Gertrude L. Thebauld* by two minutes and fifty seconds and retained the International Trophy.

The *Bluenose*, however, was a working schooner and when not in International Races was fishing off the Grand Banks. Her principal owners were E. Fenwick Zwicker, Arthur Zwicker and Angus Walters. In 1938 a Committee for the Preservation of the *Bluenose* was set up but their attempts to raise money were unsuccessful. In August, 1941, the vessel was bought by Angus Walters and a year later sold to the West Indies Trading Company. She was lost off Haiti on January 29, 1946.

The *Canadia* was one of a number of Nova Scotia vessels that raced against the *Bluenose* in the Nova Scotia Fleet Races in 1921 and 1922. In two separate races the *Canadia* came second. The vessel was registered at La Have until 1925 when she was transferred to Lunenburg. Later that year her name was changed to *Fishborn*. On December 26, 1926, the vessel ran ashore and became a total loss.

Bluenose and *Canadia* are shown here racing in Halifax Harbour in 1921. *Bluenose* (No. 2) has the lead.

BLUENOSE   Schooner   99 Tons
Built in 1921 at Lunenburg by Smith and Rhuland
Designed by William Roue
Dimensions: 130.2' x 27.1' x 10.1'
Cost of building: $35,580.00[1]
Port of Registry: Lunenburg
Owners: The Bluenose Schooner Co.

CANADIA   Schooner   130 Tons
Built in 1921 at Shelburne by Joseph McGill
Dimensions: 127.4' x 25.2' x 12.3'
Cost of building: $35,000.00[2]
Port of Registry: La Have
Owners: Canadia Ltd.

The Bluenose and the Canadia

Courtesy of Mr. Maurice Crosby,
Halifax, N.S., and Longman Canada
Ltd., Toronto, Ont.

211

The Rumrunner I'm Alone

The *I'm Alone*, a schooner of 205 tons, was built at Lunenburg by Smith & Rhuland in 1923. She represents one of the hundreds of knockabout schooners, many of which by this time were equipped with gasoline engines. She was owned by the I'm Alone Shipping Company which was in fact a cover for a group of American rumrunners. In 1929 the vessel, under the command of Captain Jack Randall, sparked off an international incident between Canada and the United States.

A Canadian Navy officer during World War I, Randall had begun his bootlegging activities in 1922 and joined the *I'm Alone* in November 1926. Although the vessel had changed owners several times, she was already well known by the American authorities as a notorious rumrunner.

The schooner left Halifax on November 4, 1928, for St. Pierre and Miquelon and collected a full cargo of liquor, which was delivered to a motor cruiser off the Louisiana coast. Afterwards she continued to make regular trips out of Belize. However, she had been spotted by a lookout craft posted by the United States Coast Guard, but disguised as a small, dirty fishing schooner.

On March 20, 1929, she was stopped by the United States Coast Guard cutter *Walcott* and ordered to surrender. Randall refused, claiming they were outside territorial waters. The *Walcott* withdrew but returned later in the day and again demanded that they heave to. When they refused, the *Walcott* opened fire. Captain Randall was shot in the leg, but he soon realized that the cutter was using wax bullets.

During the following day they were trailed by the *Walcott*, and on the morning of March 22 the United States Coast Guard cutter *Dexter*, under the command of Captain Powell, arrived on the scene. The *I'm Alone* was, at the time, about 200 miles off the American coast in the Gulf of Mexico.

Captain Powell immediately gave orders for the *I'm Alone* to heave to. When Captain Randall refused, the cutter opened fire at a range of less than 200 yards. Randall immediately hoisted the British flag! At first, the cutter directed her fire into the rigging and superstructure of the schooner. On the second ultimatum, Randall again refused and the fire was directed below the water line. Within a few minutes the *I'm Alone* sank. All of the crew escaped except the boatswain who was drowned, although his body was recovered. Captain Randall and his crew were taken to New Orleans and jailed. After a few days, however, the case was dropped and they were released.

The *Dexter* had been after the *I'm Alone* for a number of months. However, when caught, the *I'm Alone* was in international waters and therefore the *Dexter* had no jurisdiction over her. It was six years before the case was finally settled. The United States Government made a formal apology and paid $25,000 to the Government of Canada. An additional $25,666.50 was given to the crew of the *I'm Alone*. Randall received $7,906, and the boatswain's widow $10,000. The balance went to the rest of the crew.[3]

The I'm Alone at Lunenburg, N.S.

Schooner   205 Tons
Built in 1923 at Lunenburg, N.S.,
by Smith & Rhuland.
125.6′ x 27.0′ x 10.6′

Rigs

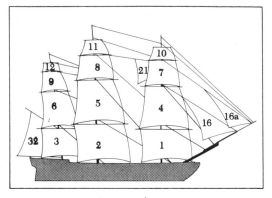

Ship, c. 1835

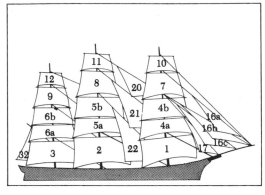

Ship, c. 1870

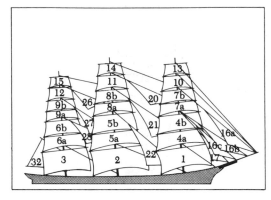

Ship, 1880

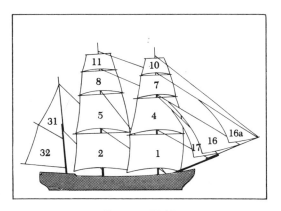

Barque, 1840

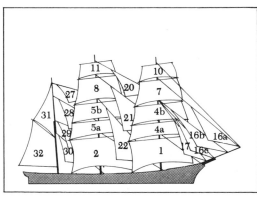

Barque, 1870

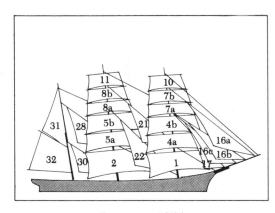

Barque, c. 1875

1. Fore sail	5. Main topsail	7. Fore topgallant	9. Mizzen topgallant
2. Main sail	5a. Main lower topsail	7a. Fore lower topgallant	9a. Mizzen lower topgallant
3. Mizzen or cross-jack	5b. Main upper topsail	7b. Fore upper topgallant	9b. Mizzen upper topgallant
4. Fore topsail	6. Mizzen topsail	8. Main topgallant	10. Fore royal
4a. Fore lower topsail	6a. Mizzen lower topsail	8a. Main lower topgallant	11. Main royal
4b. Fore upper topsail	6b. Mizzen upper topsail	8b. Main upper topgallant	12. Mizzen royal

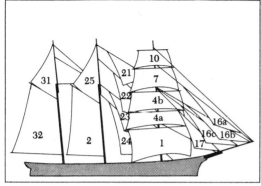

Barquentine, c. 1875

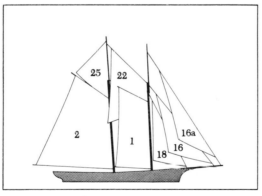

Brig, c. 1830

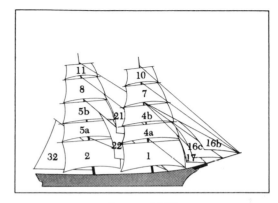

Brig, c. 1865

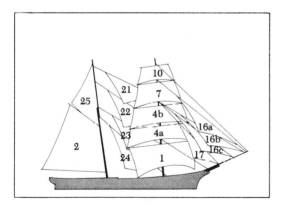

Brigantine, 1870

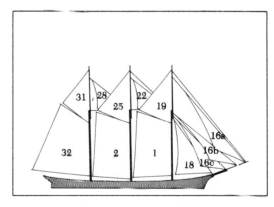

Schooner, c. 1890

Tern schooner, c. 1890

13. Fore skysail
14. Main skysail
15. Mizzen skysail
16. Jib
16a. Flying jib
16b. Outer jib
16c. Inner jib
17. Fore topmast staysail
18. Fore staysail
19. Fore gaff topsail
20. Main royal staysail
21. Main topgallant staysail
22. Main topmast staysail
23. Main head staysail
24. Main staysail
25. Main gaff topsail
26. Mizen royal staysail
27. Mizzen topgallant staysail
28. Mizzen topmast staysail
29. Mizzen head staysail
30. Mizzen staysail
31. Mizzen gaff topsail
32. Spanker

Numbers of Vessels Built

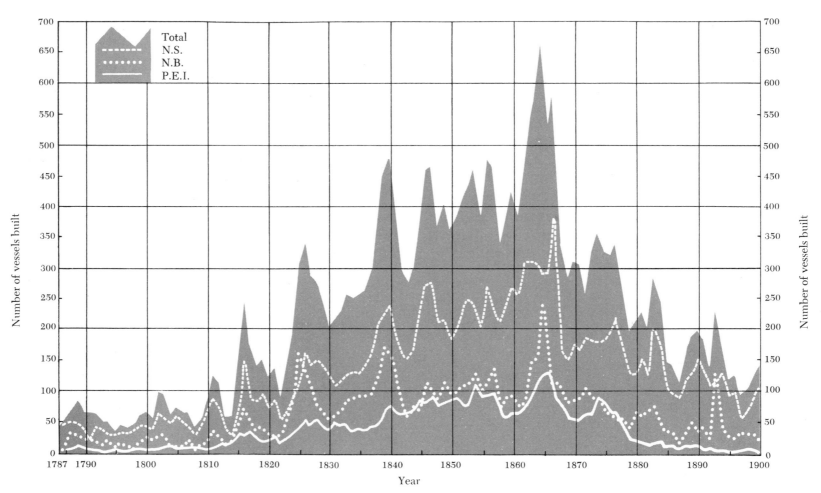

Number of vessels built and registered in the Maritime Provinces.

The figures for the table have been compiled from the following sources:

1787–1873 Great Britain — Customs Records, British Sessional Papers, Canadian Shipping Registers and Annual Lists.

1874–1900 Canada — Department of Marine and Fisheries Annual Reports.

Sources

Abbreviations:

D.U.A.	Dalhousie University Archives, Killam Memorial Library, Halifax, Nova Scotia
M.U.	Memorial University, St. John's, Newfoundland
N.S.M.	Nova Scotia Museum, Halifax, Nova Scotia
P.A.C.	Public Archives of Canada, Ottawa, Ontario
P.R.O.	Public Record Office, London, England

Introduction

1. P.R.O. BT 6 185. Courtesy of the Controller of H. M. Stationery Office.
2. Canada, Department of Marine and Fisheries, *Annual Report 1878*.

Chapter 1

1. P.R.O. CO 221, 28–31.
2. *British Sessional Papers.* 1731–1800, Vol. 17, 1786–1787, Bill No. 529, 1786.
3. P.R.O. BT 6, 192 and 193.
4. P.R.O. CO 221, 28.

Chapter 2

1. George E. E. Nichols. "Notes on Nova Scotia Privateers," p. 118.
2. D.U.A. John Harris. Journal May 22, 1813–June 30, 1813. Courtesy of Dalhousie University Library.

Chapter 3

1. David M. Williamson, "Bulk Carriers and Timber Imports," p. 374.
2. D.U.A. Thomas Colton Creighton. Diary, 1843–1846 (transcript). Courtesy of Miss Isabell Creighton.

Chapter 4

1. Howard L. Chapelle. *The Search For Speed Under Sail*, p. 398.
2. Howard L. Chapelle. *The History of the American Sailing Ships*, p. 284.
3. Ibid., p. 286.
4. David R. MacGregor, *Fast Sailing Ships 1775–1875*, p. 166.
5. Ibid., p. 164.
6. Y.C.H.S. Killam Bros. Log Book of the *S. L. Tilley*, 1856–58. Courtesy of the Yarmouth County Historical Society.
7. P.A.C. RG 12 A 1 Vol. 93, Canada, Department of Transport. Shipping Registers, Yarmouth, 1856. Courtesy of the Public Archives of Canada.
8. Ibid., Yarmouth, 1856.
9. Mrs. Arthur Moran. James H. Moran Papers. Protest of the *Beau Monde*, 1865. Courtesy of Mrs. Arthur Moran.
10. Y.C.H.S. C. F. MacMullen, List of Sailings of the *Maggie Hammond*, 1863–71. Courtesy of the Yarmouth County Historical Society.
11. Y.C.H.S. Killam Bros., Protest of the *Research*, 1866–67. Courtesy of the Yarmouth County Historical Society.
12. Miss Gwendolyn Shand. Aylward, Thomas, Note Book, 1864–86. Courtesy of Miss Gwendolyn Shand.

Chapter 5

1. Canada, Department of Marine and Fisheries. *Supplement No. 2 to the Annual Report*, 1874, pp. 465–66.
2. Ibid., *Annual Report, 1878*, pp. lxi–lxiii.
3. M.U. Great Britain, Board of Trade, Registrar General of Shipping and Seamen. Vessels' Agreements and Crew Lists, Log Book of the *Robert Godfrey*, 1869. Courtesy of the Controller of H.M. Stationery Office.

4. Charles Armour. David Taylor. Papers of Barque *Robert Godfrey*, March 2, 1869.
5. Charles Armour. David Taylor. Correspondence, March 18, 1869.
6. D.U.A. John D. MacLeod, Register of Protests of Vessels, 1867–75, p. 11. Courtesy of Dalhousie University Library.
7. D.U.A. Ibid. pp. 13–14.
8. D.U.A. Colin Campbell. Ledger, 1872–73. Courtesy of Dalhousie University Library.
9. Charles Armour. David Taylor. Correspondence, October 15, 1868.
10. Canada, Department of Marine and Fisheries. *Supplement No. 2 to the Annual Report*, 1874, p. 460.
11. N.S.M. William Lawrence. Letter Book. October 1, 1870.
12. N.S.M. William Lawrence. Vessels' Cost Accounts, 1872–1874.
13. Mrs. Harry Bannister. Hiram Palmer Papers. Protest of the *Queen of the Fleet*, 1887. Courtesy of Mrs. Harry Bannister.
14. Ibid.

15. D.U.A. James E. Dickie. Correspondence, 1856–1892. Courtesy of Dalhousie University Library.
16. Ibid., December 13, 1881.
17. Frederick William Wallace. *Wooden Ships and Iron Men*, p. 254.
18. D.U.A. Alice Coalfleet. Diary, April 6, 1892 (photocopy). Courtesy of Peter Coalfleet Dimock.
19. Ibid., 1886–1892.
20. D.U.A. Taylor Bros. Papers. 1869–1904.
21. P.A.C. RG 12 A 1 Vol. 70. Department of Transport, Shipping Registers. Parrsboro, 1861.
22. Canada, Department of Marine and Fisheries *Annual Report*, 1883, p. lxxiii.
23. P.A.C. RG 12 A 1 Vol. 329 Department of Transport, Shipping Registers, Lunenburg, 1884. Courtesy of the Public Archives of Canada.
24. D.U.A. Jonathan E. Steel. Vessels' Cost Accounts, 1884–1885. Courtesy of Dalhousie University Library.

25. Y.C.H.S. C. F. MacMullen. List of Sailings of the *County of Yarmouth*, 1884–1894. Courtesy Historical Society.
26. P.A.C. RG 12 A 1 Vol. 102, Department of Transport. Shipping Registers. Dorchester, 1885. Courtesy of the Public Archives of Canada.
27. Hector MacLeod, Liverpool, N.S. Robie MacLeod. Correspondence, Department of Marine and Fisheries to R.M. Dec. 28, 1893. Courtesy of Hector MacLeod.

Chapter 6

1. D.U.A. Bluenose Schooner Co. Minute Book, 1921 (Microfilm Copy). Original: Sherman Zwicker.
2. D.U.A. La Have Outfitting Co. Vessels' Papers, *Canadia* Accounts, 1921 (Microfilm Copy). Original: Teleen Gray.
3. Janice Patton. *The Sinking of the* I'm Alone, p. 30.

Bibliography

Manuscripts

CHARLES A. ARMOUR, Halifax, N.S.
Taylor, David. Correspondence 1868–69 and Papers of the *Robert Godfrey*, 1869.

MRS. HARRY BANNISTER, Dorchester, N.B.
Palmer, Hiram. Protest of the *Queen of the Fleet*, 1887.

BRITISH MUSEUM, London.
Liverpool Papers, 38429–38432 Vol. CCXL-CCXLIII.

DALHOUSIE UNIVERSITY ARCHIVES, Halifax, N.S.
Bluenose Schooner Co., Lunenburg, N.S. Minute Book, 1921–1942 (microfilm). Original: Sherman Zwicker, Lunenburg, N.S.
Coalfleet, Alice. Hantsport, N.S. Diary 1886–1892 (photocopy). Original: Peter Coalfleet Dimock, Windsor, N.S.

Campbell, Colin. Weymouth, N.S. Ledgers and Letter Books, 1860–1881.
Dickey, James. Upper Stewiacke, N.S. Correspondence 1856–1892.
Frieze and Roy, Maitland, N.S. Correspondence and Misc. Papers, 1839–1885.
Ham, J. Harry, Lunenburg, N.S. Sail Plans of Vessels. 1885–1910 (copies). Original: Everett Lohnes, Lunenburg, N.S.
Harris, John, Annapolis, N.S. Journal, 1813–1816.
La Have Outfitting Co., La Have, N.S. Vessels' Papers, 1921 (microfilm). Original: Mr. Teleen Gray, La Have, N.S.
MacLeod, John D., Pictou, N.S. Register of Protests of Vessels, 1867–1875.
Steel, Jonathan E., Scots Bay, N.S. Vessels' Cost Accounts, 1871–1885.

Taylor Bros., Saint John, N.B. Ledgers, Daybooks and Misc. Papers, 1870–1904.
Zwicker & Co., Lunenburg, N.S. Papers of the *Bluenose*, 1921–1942.

LIVERPOOL CUSTOM HOUSE, Liverpool, England.
Liverpool Shipping Registers, 1786–1825.
Liverpool — Subsidiary Register of Other Ports, 1786–1818.

LONDON CUSTOM HOUSE, London, England.
Greenock Shipping Registers, 1787–1825.
London Shipping Registers, 1787–1825.
Port Glasgow Shipping Registers, 1787–1825.

MRS. ARTHUR MORAN, St. Martins, N.B.
Moran, James and Moran, James H., St. Martins, N.B. Misc. Papers, 1847–1874.

MR. HECTOR MACLEOD, Liverpool, N.S.
MacLeod, Robbie, Liverpool, N.S. Correspondence, 1893.

MEMORIAL UNIVERSITY, St. John's, Nfld.
Great Britain, Board of Trade, Registrar General of Shipping and Seamen.
Vessels' Agreements and Crew Lists. Log Book of the *Robert Godfrey*, 1868–69.

NEW BRUNSWICK MUSEUM, Saint John, N.B.
Cochran, Frederick M. The History of St. Martins, New Brunswick Built Ships.
Numerous Lists of Vessels built by New Brunswick Builders.

NOVA SCOTIA MUSEUM, Halifax, N.S.
Lawrence, William D., Maitland, N.S. Letter Book and Vessels' Cost Accounts, 1870–1874.

PROVINCIAL ARCHIVES OF NEW BRUNSWICK, Fredericton, N.B.
Rex Cu, 1784–85, Custom House, Saint John, N.B. Shipping Returns.

PROVINCIAL ARCHIVES OF PRINCE EDWARD ISLAND, Charlottetown, P.E.I.
Custom House, Charlottetown, P.E.I. Shipping Returns, 1790–1811.

PUBLIC ARCHIVES OF CANADA, Ottawa, Ont.
RG 12 Department of Transport, Shipping Registers, 1787–1930.
RG 16 Department of National Revenue, Port Records, 1790–1900.

PUBLIC ARCHIVES OF NOVA SCOTIA, Halifax, N.S.
Lawrence, William D., Maitland, N.S. Plans of Vessels, 1847–1874.
Nova Scotia, Court of Vice Admiralty, Halifax, Perkins, Simeon. Diary, 1766–1812. Transcript.
N.S. Minute Books and Lists of Vessels Captured, 1749–1815.

PUBLIC RECORD OFFICE, London, England.
Great Britain, Board of Trade.
BT 6 185 State of Trade of England in Its Imports and Exports, 1697–1773.
BT 6 190 Naval Office Returns, Quebec, 1787–1794.
BT 6 191 Annual Lists for 1789.
BT 6 192 and 193 Ships Registered, 1786–1793.
BT 107 to BT 111 Registrar General of Shipping and Seamen, Shipping Registers. Transcripts and Transactions. Great Britain and Colonial Ports, 1812, 1813, 1817–1890.
BT 162 1 to 19 Registrar General of Shipping and Seamen, Annual Lists of Vessels Registered at Colonial Ports, 1791, 1792, 1807–1850.
Great Britain, Colonial Office.

CO 27, 12–15; CO 33, 18–26; CO 41, 6–12; CO 76, 4–8; CO 106, 1–8; CO 128, 1; CO 142, 17029; CO 193, 1–2; CO 221, 28–35; CO 231, 1–2; CO 259, 2–3; CO 265, 1–2; CO 290, 1–3; CO 300, 16; CO 317, 1.
Canada and West Indies, Shipping Returns, 1750–1820.

Great Britain, Customs.
Customs 17, 10–30 State of Navigation, Commerce and Revenue. 1787–1808.

Great Britain Home Office.
HO 76 1–2 Canada and West Indies, Shipping Returns. 1790–1794.

MISS GWENDOLYN SHAND, Windsor, N.S.
Aylward, Thomas, Windsor, N.S. Note Book, 1864–1886.

YARMOUTH COUNTY HISTORICAL SOCIETY, Yarmouth, N.S.
Killam Bros., Yarmouth, N.S. Protest of the *Research*, 1866–67.
———, Log Books of the *S.L. Tilley*, 1856–58.
MacMullen, C. F. List of Sailings of the *County of Yarmouth*, 1884–94 and the *Maggie Hammond*, 1863–71.

Books

BLAKELEY, PHYLLIS R. AND STEVENS, JOHN R. *Ships of the North Shore (Pictou, Colchester and Cumberland Counties)*. Halifax, N.S.: The Maritime Museum of Canada, Occasional Paper No. 11, 1963.

BACKMAN, BRIAN AND PHIL. *Bluenose*. Toronto: McClelland and Stewart, 1965.

BANK OF NOVA SCOTIA. *History of the Bank of Nova Scotia*. [Halifax], [1901].

BRITISH SESSIONAL PAPERS 1731–1800. Vol. 17, 1786–1787. Bill No. 529, 1786.
——— 1837/38. Vol. 45, p. 357.

CAMERON, JAMES M. *Ships and Seamen of New Glasgow, Nova Scotia*. (2nd printing with revisions.) New Glasgow, N.S.: The Hector Publishing Co. Ltd., August, 1959.

CAMPBELL, DUNCAN. *Nova Scotia in Its Historical, Mercantile and Industrial Relations*. Montreal: John Lovell, 1873.

CANADA, DEPARTMENT OF MARINE AND FISHERIES. *Annual Reports*. Ottawa: published by Order of Parliament, 1868–1925.
———. *List of Vessels on the Registry Books of Canada*. Ottawa: published by Order of Parliament, 1783–1925.

CHAPELLE, HOWARD I. *The History of the American Sailing Navy*. New York: Bonanza Books, 1949.
———. *The History of the American Sailing Ships*. New York: Bonanza Books, 1935.
———. *The Search for Speed Under Sail*. London, Eng.: George Allen and Unwin Ltd., 1968.

CHATTERTON, E. KEBLE. *Fore and Aft*. London, Eng.: Seeley, Service and Co. Ltd., 1912.

COUSINS, JOHN. "Those Gallant Ships." Toronto: *Canadian Antiques Collector*. Vol. 8, No. 1, 1973, pp. 58–60.

FAY, CHARLES EDEY. *Mary Celeste — The Odyssey of an Abandoned Ship*. Salem, Mass.: Peabody Museum, 1942.

FRASER, D. G. L. "The Origin and Function of the Court of Vice Admiralty in Halifax, 1749–1759." Halifax, N.S.: *Collections of the Nova Scotia Historical Society*. Vol. 33, 1961, pp. 57–80.

GREENHILL, BASIL. *The Great Migration*. London, Eng.: H.M.S.O., 1968.
———. *The Merchant Sailing Schooners*. 2 vol. Newton Abbot, England: David and Charles, 1968.
———. *The Merchant Sailing Ship*. Newton Abbot, Eng.: David and Charles, 1970.
——— AND GIFFARD, ANN. *Westcountrymen in Prince Edward's Isle*. Newton Abbot, Eng.: David and Charles; and Toronto: Toronto University Press, 1967.

LARRACEY, EDWARD W. *The First Hundred*. Moncton, N.B.: Moncton Publishing Co. Ltd., 1970.

LAWRENCE, WILLIAM D. *Untitled Pamphlet*, Maitland, N.S.: published by the Author, 1880.

LAWSON, J. MURRAY. *Record of the Shipping of Yarmouth, N.S.* Yarmouth, N.S.: published by the Author, 1876.
———. *Appendix to the Record of the Shipping of Yarmouth, N.S.* (1876–1884). Yarmouth, N.S.: *Herald* Office, 1884.

LEVER, DARCY. *The Young Officer's Sheet Anchor*. 2nd ed. London: 1819; reprint ed., New York: Edward W. Sweetman, 1955.

LUBBOCK, BASIL. *The China Clippers*. Glasgow:

Brown, Son and Ferguson, 1922.

——. *The Colonial Clippers.* Glasgow: Brown, Son and Ferguson, 1948.

——. *Last of the Windjammers.* 2 vols. Glasgow: Brown, Son and Ferguson, 1927.

MACBETH, GEORGE. *Johnny Woodboat.* Ottawa: Museum Restoration Service, 1969.

MACGREGOR, DAVID. *Fast Sailing Ships 1775–1875.* Lausanne, Switzerland: Edita, 1973.

MACMECHAN, ARCHIBALD. *Old Province Tales.* Toronto: McClelland and Stewart, [1924].

——. *Sagas of the Sea.* London, Eng.: Dent and Sons, 1923.

——. *Tales of the Sea.* Toronto: McClelland and Stewart, 1947.

——. *There Go the Ships.* Toronto: McClelland and Stewart, [1928].

MACNUTT, W. S. *New Brunswick, A History: 1784–1867.* Toronto: Macmillan, 1963.

MACHUM, LLOYD A. *A History of Moncton.* Moncton, N.B.: The City of Moncton, 1965.

MANNEY, LOUISE. *Shipbuilding in Bathurst.* Fredericton, N.B.: Brunswick Press, 1965.

——. *Ships of Kent County.* Sackville, N.B.: Tribune Press, 1949.

——. *Ships of Miramichi.* The New Brunswick Museum, Historical Studies No. 10. Saint John, N.B.: Lingley Printing Co. Ltd., 1961.

MARTIN, JOHN. *The Story of Dartmouth.* Dartmouth, N.S.: published by the Author, 1957.

MURDOCK, BEAMISH. *A History of Nova Scotia.* 3 vols. Halifax, N.S.: James Barnes, 1865.

NARES, G. S. *Seamanship.* 4th ed. Portsmouth, Eng.: James Griffin and Co. London, Eng.: Longmans, Green, Reader and Dyer, 1868.

NAVAL CHRONICLE. London, Eng.: Bunney and Gold, 5, January–July, 1801, pp. 174–5.

NEW BRUNSWICK MAGAZINE. Saint John, N.B.: William Kilby Reynolds, editor and publisher. 2, 1899, p. 279.

NICHOLS, GEORGE E. E. "Notes on Nova Scotia Privateers." *Collections of the Nova Scotia Historical Society.* Vol. 13, pp. 111–52.

PARKER, JOHN P. *Cape Breton Ships and Men.* North Sydney, N.S.: published by the Author, 1967.

——. *Sails of the Maritimes.* North Sydney, N.S.: published by the Author, 1960.

PATTERSON, FRANK H. *The Days of the Ships: Tatamagouche, N.S.* Truro, N.S.: published by the Author, 1970.

PATTERSON, GEORGE. *A History of the County of Pictou, Nova Scotia.* Montreal: Dawson, 1877.

PATTON, JANICE. *The Sinking of the I'm Alone.* Toronto: McClelland and Stewart, 1973.

PULLEN, H. F. *Atlantic Schooners.* Fredericton, N.B.: Brunswick Press, 1967.

RADDALL, THOMAS. *The Rover.* Toronto: Macmillan, 1958.

RANDELL, JACK. *I'm Alone.* Indianapolis, U.S.A.: The Bobbs-Merrill Co., 1930.

REED, THOMAS. *Seamanship.* 24th ed. Sunderland, Eng.: Thomas Reed & Co. Ltd., /n.d./

RYDER, HUIA G. *Edward John Russell, Marine Artist.* Saint John, N.B.: The New Brunswick Museum, 1953.

SPICER, STANLEY T. *Masters of Sail.* Toronto: Ryerson Press, 1968.

STEWART, GEORGE. *The Story of the Great Fire in St. John, N.B.* Toronto: Belford Brothers, 1877.

STEEL, DAVID. *Elements of Mastmaking, Sailmaking and Rigging.* (From the 1794 edition.) Reprint of the 1932 ed. New York: Edward W. Sweetman, /n.d./

STEEL, DAVID. *The Ship-Master's Assistant and Owner's Manual.* 10th ed. London: P. Steel, 1803.

TAIT, JAMES. *New Seamanship and Nautical Knowledge.* Revised by H. T. Jefferys. Reprinted. Glasgow: Brown, Son and Ferguson, 1946.

UNDERHILL, HAROLD A. *Masting and Rigging.* Glasgow: Brown, Son and Ferguson, 1958.

——. *Plank-on-Frame Models.* 2 vols. Glasgow: Brown, Son and Ferguson, 1960.

——. *Sailing Ship Rigs and Riggings.* Glasgow: Brown, Son and Ferguson, 1958.

WALLACE, FREDERICK WILLIAM. *In the Wake of the Wind Ships.* London, Eng.: Hodder and Stoughton, 1927.

——. *Record of Canadian Shipping.* Toronto: The Musson Book Co., 1929.

——. *Rovering Fisherman.* Gardenvale, P.Q.: Canadian Fisherman, 1955.

——. *Under Sail in the Last of the Clippers.* Glasgow: Brown, Son and Ferguson, 1936.

——. *Wooden Ships and Iron Men.* London, Eng.: Hodder and Stoughton, 1924.

WILLIAMS, DAVID M. "Bulk Carriers and Timber Transport: The British North American Trade and the Shipping Boom of 1824–25." *The Mariners Mirror* Vol. 54, November, 1968, pp. 373–82.

WRIGHT, ESTHER CLARK. *The Miramichi.* Sackville, N.B.: The Tribune Press, 1945.

In addition, numerous volumes of the following shipping registers were consulted:

American Lloyd's. New York: 1857– .
Bureau Veritas. Paris: 1829– .
Lloyd's Register of Shipping. London: 1760–1833.
Lloyd's Register of British and Foreign Shipping. London: 1834– .
Mercantile Navy List. London 1857– .
Record of American and Foreign Shipping. New York: 1867– .

Index